DATE DUE

APR 1 2 '89	
FEB 1 5 1991	
APR 4 1991	
MAR 2 7 1992	
JUL 5 1994	
NOV 29 1994	
APR 1 5 1996	
OCT 3 1 1996	
NOV 2 7 1996	
DEC 1 7 1996	
JAN 0 2 1997	

```
F          Miller, Ray, 1919-
387
M55        Ray Miller's Texas
1985          forts


$13.95
```

Books by Ray Miller

Texas Parks: A History and Guide
Ray Miller's Galveston
Ray Miller's Houston
Eyes of Texas Travel Guide: Panhandle/Plains Edition
Eyes of Texas Travel Guide: Fort Worth/Brazos Valley Edition
Eyes of Texas Travel Guide: Hill Country/Permian Basin Edition
Eyes of Texas Travel Guide: San Antonio/Border Edition
Eyes of Texas Travel Guide: Dallas/East Texas Edition
Eyes of Texas Travel Guide: Houston/Gulf Coast Edition

RAY MILLER'S
TEXAS FORTS

A History and Guide

RAY MILLER'S
TEXAS FORTS
A HISTORY AND GUIDE

Library of Congress Catalog Card Number 85-62841
ISBN: 0-89123-036-X

Cover Design: Ron Tammariello
Design and Production Art: Tony Romano
Chapter Openers: Graham Ward
Map: Ginny Bliss

Set in Century Book II by Diana Rankin. Printed in the
United States of America by Capital Printing, Austin.

For Shannon and Christian

CONTENTS

Foreword XI

Introduction XIII

Hostile Neighbors and the First Federal Posts 1

The Border Forts 15

The First Line of Frontier Forts 37

The Second Line and the Road West 51

The Effect of the Stage Lines and the Civil War 107

The Last Frontier Forts and the End of the Indian War 121

Later Forts 169

Appendix 179

Index 219

Acknowldegements 220

Photo Credits 222

FOREWORD

I knew Ray Miller long before he knew me. When I left Congress and moved to Houston to go into business in 1955, Ray had been a news reporter in town for 16 years. I'm happy to report that he's still going strong today.

One of the first things you learn about him is that when it comes to Texas, Ray cares. And he knows the state so very well. A few years ago, when I was trying to learn more about some of the beautiful and promising areas of Texas, one of the first people I called was this man who had, after all, written the *Eyes Of Texas Travel Guide* series, not to mention other books on Houston and Galveston and on Texas Parks.

When someone who understands Texas as well as Ray sits down to write about one of the most interesting and exciting aspects of its development, there can be no doubt the result will be superb. The story of the federal forts in Texas starts with the first one, Fort Brown — which was established at the outset of the Mexican War on the site of what is now Brownsville. It is a story that unfolds on the very edge of our western frontier. And a rough edge it was.

This combination, an author who knows his subject and a subject that contains all the elements of high drama, should prove irresistible to just about any reader.

Lloyd Bentsen
Washington, D.C.
August 1985

INTRODUCTION

Forts have been built and maintained in Texas by the Spanish and the French, the Mexicans and the Republic of Texas, the Confederacy and the United States.

This is a book about the federal forts, with emphasis on the period between 1845 and 1885. It was a time of conflict with Mexico and the Plains Indians. It was a time when the U.S. Army was obliged to keep between one-fourth and one-third of its manpower in Texas. The overland mail system was born in this period and it gave way to the transcontinental railroads in the same generation.

It was a time that had much to do with shaping the character of Texas and the nation.

The federal forts on the border and on the Indian frontier are dealt with here in more or less chronological order. Other forts, camps and presidios are described briefly in the Appendix.

Ray Miller
Houston
August 1985

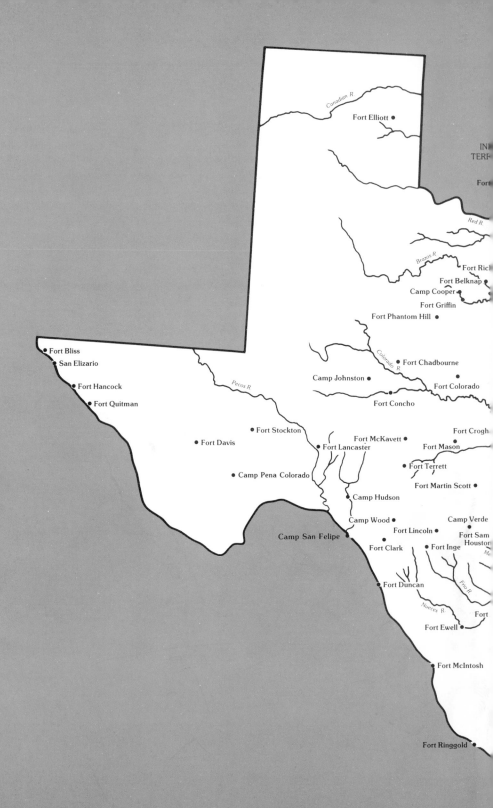

Fort Elliott •

IN[
TERF

Fort

Red R.

Canadian R.

Brazos R.

Fort Ric[

Fort Belknap •

Camp Cooper •

Fort Griffin •

Fort Phantom Hill •

Colorado R.

Fort Chadbourne •

Camp Johnston •

Fort Colorado •

Fort Concho •

• Fort Bliss

• San Elizario

Pecos R.

• Fort Hancock

• Fort Quitman

• Fort Stockton

Fort Crogh[

Fort McKavett •

Fort Mason •

• Fort Davis

• Fort Lancaster

Fort Terrett •

• Camp Pena Colorado

Fort Martin Scott •

• Camp Hudson

Camp Wood •

Camp Verde •

Fort Lincoln •

Fort Sam Houston •

Camp San Felipe •

Fort Clark •

• Fort Inge

Me[

• Fort Duncan

Frio R.

Nueces R.

Fort

Fort Ewell •

• Fort McIntosh

Fort Ringgold •

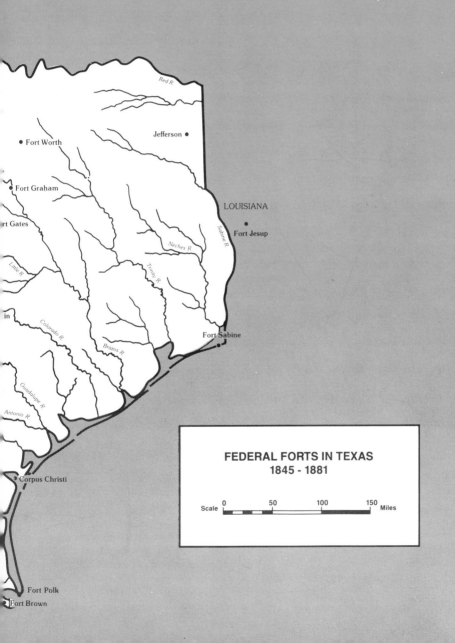

Red R.

Jefferson ●

● Fort Worth

● Fort Graham

LOUISIANA

rt Gates

● Fort Jesup

Neches R.

Little R.

Sabine R.

Trinity R.

in

Colorado R.

Brazos R.

Fort Sabine

Guadalupe R.

Antonio R.

● Corpus Christi

Fort Polk

Fort Brown

FEDERAL FORTS IN TEXAS
1845 - 1881

Scale 0   50   100   150 Miles

HOSTILE NEIGHBORS AND THE FIRST FEDERAL POSTS

From the beginning of Anglo Texas until
1875, the Comanches were the principal and
most stubborn adversaries Texans had.

— W.W. Newcomb, Jr.,
The Indians of Texas

A large part of the territory Texas claimed was occupied by Indians and part of it was claimed by the Mexicans when Texas joined the United States in 1845. The Indians Texans feared most were the Apaches, the Kiowas and especially the Comanches.

The Comanches got here before the Anglos did but they were not native Texans. They were an unpopular branch of the Shoshoni tribe. *Comanche* means enemy in the Ute language. The Comanches came down from the northern plains in about 1700 and made the discovery that transformed them from an undistinguished band of nomads into the lords of the High Plains. The discovery was the horse.

The Spanish brought horses from Europe to Mexico in the 1520s. The Apaches occupied the High Plains section of what is now Texas before the Comanches came. The Apaches had probably come to Texas from the Pacific Northwest sometime before 1500. The Comanches pushed them into far west Texas and New Mexico during the 1700s. The Kiowas and the Kiowa Apaches fought against the Comanches, but they became allies by the 1850s. W.W. Newcomb, Jr. suggests in *The Indians of Texas* that the Kiowas were descended from some Pueblo tribe. Their culture was a little more sophisticated than that of the other Plains Indians.

Some of the Apaches had acquired horses by 1700. The Comanches took their horses and drove the Apaches off the plains. The Comanches were at war continuously from that time until Colonel Ranald Mackenzie got the best of Quanah Parker in Palo Duro Canyon in 1874. The Spanish had lost control of Texas to the Republic of Mexico in 1821 and the Anglos ousted the Mexicans in 1836. But the Indians still controlled vast stretches of west and northwest Texas.

The Comanches mastered horsemanship like no other people in history. Horses were their livelihood and their currency. They lived on horseback, following the buffalo and raiding settlements far south of the Rio Grande to get more horses.

One reason the Spanish agreed to let Anglos settle in Texas was their fear of the Comanches. They hoped the Anglo settlements would absorb some of the energies of the Comanches. This happened to some extent, but the Comanches continued to raid south of the Rio Grande too. Stephen F. Austin established the Texas Rangers in the 1820s to cope with the Comanches. But the Rangers were on the defensive most of the time until Sam Colt's new revolver reached the frontier in 1839 and evened the odds.

The Comanches were fighting for their way of life in their final years on the plains in the early 1870s. They fought for personal glory before that and they stole horses as much for status as for profit. These Indians had no history of aggression before they discovered horses. They developed a culture suited to the new status their mastery of horsemanship gave them. Their chiefs usually were respected senior members of the tribe. They made some decisions about when and where to move the camps but their decisions were never really law. Individual Comanches in disagreement with their chiefs' decisions could and did transfer to another band. They never felt bound by any treaty a chief agreed to.

The Comanche war chiefs were braves with confidence and leadership ability. Almost any Comanche brave could propose a raid. Other braves would join in if they

President Polk's war with Mexico was popular in Texas but unpopular with most Americans. General Zachary Taylor's brisk and aggressive conduct of the campaign won him a big personal following and helped him get elected president in 1850.

thought the prospects were good. The leader was the absolute boss during a raiding expedition and he divided up the spoils. W.W. Newcomb says that the war chiefs usually were generous in their division of the stolen goods and livestock. This made it easier for them to get recruits for the next raid. And the glory was more important than the booty, anyway, in their scheme of things. Comanche warriors gained status by stealing horses, killing enemies at close range and collecting scalps. The greater the risk, the more status.

The Texas Indians were a purely Texas problem until July 4, 1845, when Texans ratified the Joint Resolution of the United States Congress, providing for the an-

nexation of Texas. The formalities were not all completed until December 29, but the United States Army moved immediately after July 4 to accept responsibility for defending Texas. There were 8349 officers and men in the United States Army at the time and it is doubtful whether any of them had any idea what defending Texas would involve.

It was well understood in Washington that Mexico still disputed Texas' claim of independence and especially disputed Texas' claim to the territory between the Nueces River and the Rio Grande where much of the land was owned by Mexican nationals. Anson Jones was president of the Republic of Texas at the time of annexation. He claimed that President James K. Polk of the United States was determined to have a war with Mexico. Jones said Polk tried to get him to start it.

The Joint Resolution pledged the United States government to adjust all questions of boundary that might arise with other governments. U.S. General Zachary Taylor had an army camped in Louisiana, near Fort Jessup, just outside Texas' eastern border when Texas ratified the Joint Resolution. Taylor had the 3rd and 4th Infantry Regiments and seven companies of the 2nd Dragoons in what was being called the Army of Observation.

This army was to be the instrument for adjusting the boundary dispute and for creating some new boundaries where there had been no dispute.

Taylor and his army started moving as soon as the annexation was ratified. General David Twiggs and the 2nd Dragoons rode across the border into Texas. General Taylor and his staff and the infantry went down to New Orleans and sailed from there on the steamboat *Alabama* on July 23. It apparently was left up to Zachary Taylor to decide where his base in Texas should be. He chose the village of Corpus Christi at the eastern edge of the disputed area. His troops set up a tent city. Later ships brought more infantry and some artillery. There was considerable drilling and train-

The first real battle of the Mexican War was fought May 8, 1846, on the Texas side of the Rio Grande. Zachary Taylor and about 2000 Americans clashed with a Mexican force about twice as large. The battle was fought near this site, 5½ miles north of Brownsville on Farm Road 1847. The Americans won.

ing at this post. Taylor called it Fort Marcy for Secretary of War William Marcy. There were no fortifications at Fort Marcy and it never became a permanent post, but it was the first military establishment in Texas to display the flag of the United States. The date the first units arrived was July 27, 1845.

Taylor got orders while he was at Fort Marcy to choose and occupy a position on the Rio Grande. He was given authority to decide after he got there whether the

defense of Texas required crossing the Rio Grande. He was also authorized to call upon Texas and Louisiana for volunteers to serve with him.

General Taylor left Corpus Christi for the Rio Grande in early March, 1846, with 307 wagons, 1900 horses and 50 ox teams. This force arrived on the bank of the Rio Grande opposite the city of Matamoros on March 28, 1846, and planted the U.S. flag to show that the boundry question had been adjusted.

General Taylor left the main body of his army camped opposite Matamoros. He and a few units went down to the mouth of the Rio Grande to set up a supply base to receive the shipments that would be coming to him by sea. He named this temporary base Fort Polk for the president and returned to the camp opposite Matamoros where he had his troops build a system of earthworks and install some cannon. These guns were trained on the city of Matamoros by April 5 and the Mexicans were building fortifications on their side of the river. Mexican President Mariano Paredes y Arrillaga had declared Mexico in a state of defensive war by April 23. Some of Taylor's men got into a skirmish with Mexican soldiers on the Texas side of the river on April 25. Sixteen Americans were killed. President Polk's case was made. He asked Congress for a formal declaration of war on May 11 and Congress quickly complied.

There had been two more fights by then. General Taylor had decided early in May to go back down to Fort Polk to strengthen that base. He left 250 troops at the main camp opposite Matamoros. This camp was informally being called Fort Taylor by this time. Taylor left Major Jacob Brown in command. The Mexicans shelled the fort. A shell fragment hit Major Brown. The post doctor amputated his leg.

General Taylor had to fight his way back from Fort Polk to Fort Taylor. He defeated a Mexican force at Palo Alto on May 8 and again at Resaca de la Palma on May 9.

Major Brown died of his wounds and the attentions of the Army medicos on May 9. The rude fort opposite Matamoros was renamed in his honor. It became Fort Brown on May 17, 1846. The fort served mostly as a supply base during the war with Mexico.

General Taylor's little army defeated the same Mexican army, commanded by General Mariano Arista, on May 9, a little closer to Brownsville at Resaca de la Palma. Arista retired to the Mexican side of the Rio Grande. Taylor soon followed.

The Mexican War achieved every objective President Polk could have hoped for, and most of what several U.S. presidents before him had dreamed of. U.S. troops occupied Mexico City and the Mexicans agreed to peace terms in 1848. They renounced all claims to Texas and recognized the Rio Grande as the boundary and ceded to the United States most of the territory between Texas and the Pacific Coast. The United States agreed to pay Mexico $15 million and agreed the following year to pay the state of Texas $10 million for giving up its claim to parts of New Mexico and Colorado. It was a bargain as a real estate deal. But there was a clause in the treaty ending the war with Mexico that put the United States under a continuing and awkward obligation.

> "Considering that a great part of the territories which by the present treaty are to be comprehended for the future within the limits of the United States is now occupied by savage tribes, who will hereafter be under the exclusive control of the government of the United States and whose incursions within the territory of Mexico would be prejudicial in the extreme, it is solemnly agreed that all such incursions shall be forcibly restrained by the government of the United States whensoever this may be necessary; and that when they cannot be prevented, they shall be punished by the said government, and satisfaction for the same shall be exacted, all in the same way and with equal diligence and energy, as if the same incursions were meditated or committed within its own territory, against its own citizens."
>
> *Article XI, Treaty of Guadalupe Hidalgo, May 30, 1848*

The U.S. Army gained a new appreciation of horse soldiers from the experience of collaborating with well-armed Texas Rangers.

Gold was discovered in California in 1849, right after it became a U.S. Territory. Americans began swarming westward. Thousands of them came across Texas and they expected protection from the hostile Indians.

The United States Army was suddenly saddled with the job of protecting a thousand miles of border and a thousand miles of Indian frontier. The Army had been

expanded to almost 47,000 men during the war with Mexico. But President Polk and Congress thought 10,000 soldiers should be enough to keep the peace after 1848.

There never were enough soldiers to do the job and few people in Washington really understood what the job on the frontier involved. The War Department kept sending infantry to man posts on the border and the frontier.

The U.S. Army had three mounted units at the time of the Mexican War. They were the 1st and 2nd Dragoons and the Mounted Rifles. But there was no real strategy for using the horsemen. Volunteer Texas Rangers did much of the scouting for the Army in the Mexican War.

Dragoons were stationed at a few of the early forts in Texas and the 2nd Cavalry took over several of the frontier posts after 1855. But most of the load fell on the infantry units. Not until 1850 were the foot soldiers furnished with some mules to ride. Infantrymen on mules were a joke to the Indians. But infantry cost less than cavalry.

The Army uniform of the period was blue wool, summer or winter. It was too warm for Texas summers and not warm enough for Texas winters. James Merrill says in *Spurs to Glory* that the mounted units on the frontier wore a lot of non-regulation clothing: white trousers and sombreros in the summer; caps of wolfskin, jackets of

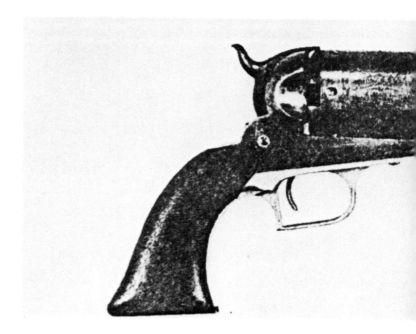

deerskin and trousers of buffalo hide in the winter.

The weapons of the mounted units after the Mexican War officially were Sharps rifles and Colt revolvers. But the Army was still using assorted flintlocks, Harper's Ferry Rifles, Hall breechloaders and single-shot horse pistols too. The forts usually had a howitzer or two.

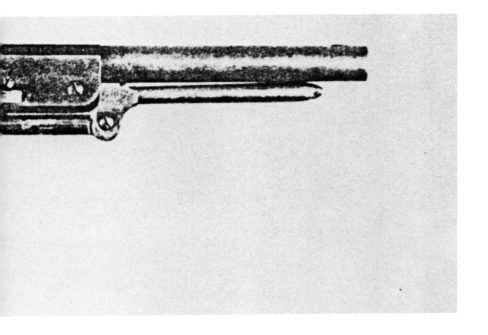

The revolver Ranger Captain Sam Walker helped Sam Colt design became the standard weapon of the U.S. Dragoons after the Mexican War.

The soldiers' pay was a scandal. Privates in the Dragoons were being paid eight dollars a month at the time the forts were being established on the Texas frontier in the 1850s. Colonels were paid $75 a month until they got a raise to $95 in 1857. There were no pensions. Congress wouldn't consider them, for fear civil servants would want them too. Officers couldn't afford to retire. So they stayed on, blocking promotions for other officers down the line. Many promising officers just resigned rather than spend 20 to 30 years working up to the rank of major.

General David Twiggs was named commander of the Department of the West at the end of the war with Mexico. State troops had been defending the Indian frontier while the army concentrated its efforts in Mexico. The state troops were discharged at the end of the war in 1848 and General Twiggs began assigning federal troops to protect the frontier and the border.

General William Jenkins Worth, commander of the Department of Texas, was named commander of the Post of San Antonio in December, 1848. He and General Twiggs, commander of the Department of the West, oversaw the establishment of the early federal forts in Texas.

There was no federal fort in San Antonio until 1876, but San Antonio was headquarters and the supply base for the federal forces in Texas almost from the start. The Army took over the Alamo and built a new roof on it and used it for years as a quartermaster depot. But the army never had title to the Alamo. The commanding officer's headquarters were in a rented building at the corner of Houston and St. Mary's streets. The military establishment here was known simply as the Post of San Antonio. General William Jenkins Worth was named commander of the post in December of 1848. The commander of the Post of San Antonio was also commander of the Department of Texas then and for a number of years afterward. General Twiggs and General Worth presided over the establishment of the early federal forts in Texas.

The Post of San Antonio had been established in 1845. The Army established posts in Austin and Corpus Christi about the same time and the headquarters of the Department of Texas moved to Austin, once, and to Corpus Christi, briefly, but returned to San Antonio both times. No permanent posts were built in Austin or Corpus Christi.

Work on the wagon roads to the west got started in earnest in 1848. Ranger John Ford and Indian Agent Robert Neighbors established a road between Austin and El Paso. Lieutenant William Whiting and Lieutenant William Smith of the Army surveyed a road from San Antonio to El Paso. Four thousand immigrants with 1200 wagons were waiting at El Paso at one time for guides to help them get to California.

El Paso was not a town yet. The immigrant traffic gave it its start and hastened development of the federal fort system.

Fort Brown
Fort Ringgold
Fort McIntosh
Fort Duncan
Fort Bliss
Post of San Elizario

THE BORDER FORTS

FORT BROWN

*Downtown Brownsville,
adjacent to International
Bridge U.S. 77,
Cameron County.*

The Army started transforming Fort Brown from a wartime encampment into a permanent base in 1848. It was a showplace by 1850. The village of Brownsville, outside the gate, was becoming a town. The Army thought there were more urgent problems elsewhere. The troops were transferred. Fort Brown was abandoned.

This opened the door to Juan Cortinas. He was a member of a wealthy, landed Mexican family, completely at home on either side of the border. Anglos regarded him as a rustler and bandit. Members of his own class in Mexico considered him a renegade, but he was very popular with poorer Mexicans. Yankee shysters had done some border Mexicans out of their property. Many Mexicans on both sides of the border had strong feelings about this. It wasn't difficult for Cortinas to get people to join him in getting even with the Yankees.

Cortinas and his crew occupied Fort Brown September 28, 1859, and took over the town of Brownsville. Five citizens were killed in the fighting that attended this maneuver. Cortinas pulled out after a few days and the U.S. troops returned. But Cortinas continued to raid settlements and steal cattle in the neighborhood until 1860 when Lieutenant Colonel Robert E. Lee came down from San Antonio to explain to the Mexican authorities that if they couldn't get Cortinas under control, he would. Lee was acting commander of the U.S. Army's Department of Texas at the time. Cortinas moved farther up the river and continued to be a problem for the guardians of the frontier periodically into the 1870s.

Fort Brown was surrendered to the Confederates in 1861. They burned it just before the Union army took it back in November of 1863.

The Confederates re-took the fort in July of 1864 and held it until the end of the war.

The U.S. Army returned to Fort Brown in 1867. The fort occupied 358 acres. Ownership of the land had been in dispute since 1853. The government finally paid $160,000 in 1895 to settle all the claims and cover the rent back to 1846.

The French had invaded Mexico during our Civil War. They installed Archduke Maximilian of Austria as emperor in 1864.

The United States was too busy with the war to do anything about the French invasion until 1866. Washington demanded then that the French troops get out of Mexico. The bristling U.S. military presence on the border underscored the demand. The French troops left Mexico in the spring of 1867. Mexican partisans captured Maximilian and executed him on June 19. Benito Juarez was restored to the presidency of Mexico and the U.S. Army command decided that Fort Brown had served its purpose. The fort was closed.

The troops were back again before the end of 1867. The Army started building new permanent buildings in 1868. Cortinas was back in action and bandits and rustlers were the main problem on the border through the 1870s. President Rutherford B. Hayes authorized the commander of the Department of Texas to pursue bandits across the Rio Grande if necessary, and this happened several times.

The black troops the Army stationed at some Texas forts after the Civil War were not well received in Brownsville. Black troops of the 25th Infantry resented the rigid

The old Fort Brown hospital building is being used now by Texas Southmost College. Several other fort buildings are still standing and being used by the college and the city. Fort Brown gave Brownsville its start.

segregation. There were several incidents over the years and on August 13, 1906, some of the black troops went into town looking for a showdown. The shooting that followed left a bartender dead and a police lieutenant wounded. Army authorities never could determine which soldiers had staged the raid. They recommended that all the men in all three companies stationed at Fort Brown be dismissed from the service. President Theodore Roosevelt approved that recommendation. All 160 men were dismissed and the Army closed the fort that fall.

Troops returned to the fort in 1913 when Mexico's internal troubles spilled over the border. The fort was expanded during World War II and then closed permanently as soon as the war ended. The government transferred the property to the city of Brownsville and Texas Southmost College.

FORT RINGGOLD

*Rio Grande City, U.S. 83 East,
Starr County.*

Fort Brown was the busiest and most important post on the border for a long time. But the army was very soon setting up more posts to guard the border and the frontier.

Units of the 1st Cavalry led by Captain J.H. Lamotte established Camp Ringgold October 26, 1848, beside the Rio Grande in what is now Starr County. Major David Ringgold was one of the officers killed in the first battle of the Mexican War at Palo Alto, May 8, 1846. The post named for the major was put at this site because this was as far up the river as steamboats could come. Henry Clay Davis had just established a town at nearby Rio Grande City and it was becoming an important port and trading center.

The name was changed from Camp Ringgold to Ringgold Barracks in July of 1849. The early buildings were frame and adobe. The most strenuous action here was

President Grant's secretary of war once threatened to close Fort Ringgold. Secretary William W. Belknap thought the white citizens of Rio Grande City were harrassing the black soldiers of the 9th Cavalry.

generated by Mexican bandit Juan Cortinas' forays across the border in the 1850s.

The post was abandoned briefly in 1859 and then reoccupied in time to be yielded to the Confederates in 1861. U.S. troops returned to Ringgold in 1869 and began building permanent brick buildings. The name was changed from Ringgold Barracks to Fort Ringgold in 1875. The fort was in continuous use until the end of World War II when it was declared surplus property.

Professional contractors built the later improvements here and at most of the other federal posts. But the early buildings often were built by the troops themselves and there were cases where officers paid out of their own pockets to have shelters built. The Army directed the post commanders in 1851 to have their troops start vegetable gardens to keep the food bills down. The gardens were successful at some posts and not successful at others. The garden at Ringgold was a failure.

William Leckie says in *The Buffalo Soldiers* that Secretary of War William Belknap threatened to withdraw federal troops from the border in the 1870s because citizens were mistreating them. Black troopers of the 9th Cavalry were ambushed by bandits near Fort Ringgold in 1875. Two of the troopers and two or three bandits were killed. The cavalrymen arrested several men near the scene the following day. Two of the suspects had gunshot wounds. They were handed over to civil authorities and

indicted for murder. One of the men went to trial and was promptly acquitted.

The grand jury went into session again and returned indictments against the regiment's commander and a lieutenant and three troopers, charging them with murder. All five men eventually were acquitted, but Leckie says they had to pay their own legal bills. The case didn't improve relations between the cavalrymen and the people they were trying to protect.

The threat to withdraw the troops never was carried out, but the 9th Cavalry was later transferred to New Mexico and was succeeded at Fort Ringgold by the (white) 8th Cavalry.

The Rio Grande School District now owns Fort Ringgold.

FORT McINTOSH

*West end of Washington Street,
Laredo, Webb County.*

U.S. troops had spent a little time on the upper Rio Grande during the Mexican War but there was no post above Ringgold until Fort McIntosh was established at Laredo on March 3, 1849.

Laredo was an old Mexican town and some of the Mexican residents did not care to be protected by the U.S. Army. Some of them moved across the river and started the town of Nuevo Laredo.

The fort was first named Camp Crawford. The name was changed to Fort McIntosh January 7, 1850, to honor Lieutenant Colonel James McIntosh of the 5th

Infantry. He had been killed at the Battle of Molino del Rey in 1847. The early federal forts in Texas were named for heroes of the Mexican War more often than not. The first units stationed here were from the 1st Infantry. The first commanding officer was Lieutenant Egbert Viele. The original fort was a system of earthworks. The post was abandoned in 1858. Two companies of the 1st Infantry returned in 1859 and left again in 1861. U.S. troops began building permanent buildings when they returned

Top: Educational institutions on the border have profited handsomely from the Army's real estate. Laredo Junior College occupies old Fort McIntosh. Voters in the Laredo school district created the junior college when the Army left Fort McIntosh at the end of World War II. The school cashed in on the G.I. education boom.

Opposite: Four of the buildings of old Fort McIntosh are occupied by the Nuevo Santander Museum. Neuvo Santander was the name of the Spanish province originally established here in the 1700s by Jose de Escandon.

to the post in 1868. The Army bought the site from the city of Laredo in 1875 and continued to add more buildings through World War II. Some of our mechanized cavalry trained at Fort McIntosh for the war in Europe.

The post was declared surplus and turned over to Laredo Junior College in 1946.

Drawing of Fort Duncan as seen from the Mexican side of the Rio Grande, probably in the late 1850s.

FORT DUNCAN

Farm Road 1021, South Eagle Pass, Maverick County.

This post was part of the border system and also the southernmost post in the original chain of frontier forts. It was established March 27, 1849, on the Rio Grande opposite Piedras Negras. It was named for Colonel James Duncan of the Inspector General's Department. The original garrison was composed of three companies of the 1st Infantry commanded by Captain Sidney Burbank. Black soldiers of the 9th Cavalry were stationed here when the U.S. Army reoccupied the post after the Civil War.

Captain John Bullis, Lieutenant Colonel William Shafter and Colonel Ranald Mackenzie made several sallies into Mexico from here, chasing Indians.

The buildings at Fort Duncan were built with native sandstone. Construction started in 1850 and this was one of the bases where the officers and some non-commissioned officers paid to have quarters built for them.

The land the Army chose for the post turned out to be owned by John Twohig of San Antonio. He tolerated the troops for five years and let them build several buildings before he negotiated a lease with the government. The rent was $1560 a

year but it almost certainly went unpaid during the Civil War years when the U.S. troops were gone and the Confederates occupied the post.

The Army abandoned the post in 1883 but then established a cavalry outpost on the property in 1891. That post was called Camp Eagle Pass. It was an outpost of Fort Clark. The government finally bought the property in 1894 but it was not used much after the border troubles died down in 1916. The property was transferred to the city of Eagle Pass in 1938. It is now a city park.

The city of Eagle Pass owns Fort Duncan now. It is a park. There is a museum in the old headquarters building.

FORT BLISS

*Pershing Drive, off U.S. 54,
northeast El Paso,
El Paso County.*

There was no town when federal troops came here the first time during the Mexican War. The city on the other side of the Rio Grande was known then as El Paso del Norte. The name was changed to Juarez in 1882.

The Army ordered a post established opposite El Paso del Norte in 1848. But it wasn't until September 14, 1849, that the troops arrived. The troops were six companies of the 3rd Infantry led by Major Jefferson Van Horne. Their march from

General John J. Pershing had an aggressive young lieutenant as his aide when he was chasing Pancho Villa in Mexico. The lieutenant was George Patton.

San Antonio was also an exploration of the road that was to play a major role in the development of the West. Van Horne had 257 soldiers, 275 wagons and 2500 head of livestock. They were a hundred days on the road. Many immigrants and gold-seekers traveled with them.

The United States and Texas had not yet settled on a boundary line between Texas and New Mexico so it was not certain which state the new Army post was in. But Texans always considered it part of Texas. There were just three ranches and a mill before Van Horne and his troops arrived here. Van Horne rented some land on what was known as Smith's Ranch. The first buildings were barracks and corrals built with adobe, about where Santa Fe and Main streets intersect, in what is now downtown El Paso.

There were enough people in the vicinity by 1850 to justify a post office. Storekeeper Franklin Coons was named postmaster and the settlement was named

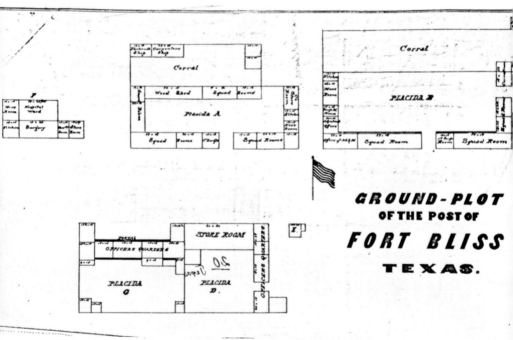

GROUND-PLOT
OF THE POST OF
FORT BLISS
TEXAS.

Wholesale improvisation was the theme of the Army's building program in the early days in Texas. This plan probably was drawn after the fort was built, rather than before. This is probably the second Fort Bliss.

Franklin. The name was changed to El Paso in 1873.

The post was abandoned as an economy measure during the Millard Fillmore administration in 1851. The troops moved to Fort Fillmore in New Mexico.

Franklin Pierce became president in 1853. He named Jefferson Davis secretary of war. Davis had been in Texas during the Mexican War. He had a great deal more interest in this part of the world than anyone in the Fillmore administration. One of Jefferson Davis' objectives was to get a transcontinental railroad built along a southern route. Davis engineered the purchase of what is now southern New Mexico and Arizona from Mexico in December of 1853 as part of this scheme. This was the transaction known as the Gadsen purchase. One of the articles in the agreement cancelled the article in the Treaty of Guadalupe Hidalgo that had obliged the United States to keep the Indians from raiding across the Rio Grande. But no border forts were closed. Davis established some additional forts on the frontier and re-established the post opposite El Paso del Norte.

The post had a new location, on land rented from James Magoffin at what was known as Magoffinsville. The new garrison arrived in January of 1854; four companies of the 8th Infantry commanded by Major Edmund Alexander. The name of the post was changed to Fort Bliss on March 8, 1854, to honor Colonel William

The citizens of El Paso built a replica of the original Fort Bliss in 1948 on the grounds of the present Fort Bliss. The replica is a free museum. The wagon in the foreground is an authentic Army wagon.

W.S. Bliss. He had been General Zachary Taylor's chief of staff during the Mexican War.

James Longstreet was in command here in 1855. He was a major then. Another future Confederate general was stationed here for a while the same year. He was Lieutenant Colonel John Bankhead Magruder.

The garrison here did some skirmishing with Apaches, provided protection for travelers and escorts for the commission surveying the boundary with New Mexico and the party surveying the route for the southern transcontinental railroad.

Fort Bliss was abandoned to the Confederates in 1861 and they burned it when they left in July of 1862. Union troops occupied Franklin and vicinity during the remainder of the Civil War.

The Army established a new post in 1868 on rented land on Stephenson's Ranch and called it Camp Concordia. The camp was re-named Fort Bliss in March of 1869. It was abandoned in January of 1877 and the adobe buildings were in poor condition by the time the Army decided to re-establish the post in 1878. The garrison occupied rented buildings for three years and then moved to a site the government had bought

Nothing is left of the first three forts the Army built here. This much is left of the fourth fort. These two apartment houses in the 1800 block of West Paisana Drive were officers' quarters when Fort Bliss was at this (Hart's Mill) site, 1881-1893.

Fort Bliss has been the Army's Air Defense Center since 1957. German rocket expert Werner Von Braun set up shop here right after World War II and continued his experiments under new management. One of Van Braun's old V-2 rockets decorates the parking lot outside the buildings where the West German army's air defense crews live when they are training here. The first experimental rocket fired by the Fort Bliss team went way off course and landed in a cemetery in Juarez.

at Hart's Mill. The post at this site was named Fort Bliss when the buildings were completed in 1881. It was the fourth site the Army had occupied here, the third one to be named Fort Bliss and the first one the government owned. Congress authorized the Rio Grande and El Paso Railroad to build tracks through the post so the Army was soon looking for another site.

Congress appropriated money for a new fort in 1890. The people of El Paso raised money to help buy the site on La Noria Mesa, just northeast of town. A new Fort Bliss was built. It has been occupied continuously since October, 1893.

Texas volunteers occupied the post during the Spanish-American War in 1898, while the Army troops went to Cuba. The 8th Infantry and General John J. Pershing were here during the turmoil in Mexico between 1914 and 1916. Pershing led an expedition into Mexico in 1916 to try to punish Pancho Villa for attacking American towns.

Fort Bliss has been at the present site since 1893. Some of the original buildings here are still in use. The monument on the parade ground is the one originally erected in the New Orleans cemetery where William W.S. Bliss was buried when he died in 1853. The monument was moved here in 1955 when Bliss' remains were moved to the National Cemetery in El Paso.

The 15th Cavalry, the 82nd Field Artillery, the 5th Cavalry, the 7th Cavalry, the 11th Cavalry and the 13th Cavalry trained at Fort Bliss and at a temporary annex called Camp Stewart during World War I.

The fort was a cavalry base until the 1940s. The 1st Cavalry Division was mechanized here before it was sent to the South Pacific in World War II. Fort Bliss became an artillery base at that time. Captured German military rockets were brought here for study at the end of World War II. The first American-made military rocket was fired here. Bliss was designated the U.S. Army Air Defense Center in 1957.

The Army sent a few airplanes to Fort Bliss in 1919 to patrol the border. The airfield established to service them was named Biggs Field for Lieutenant James Biggs of El Paso. He was one of the flyers killed in France in World War I. The field was expanded in 1941 to train bomber crews for World War II. Biggs was headquarters for the 2nd Air Force and it became Biggs Air Force Base in 1947. It has been Biggs Army Airfield since the Air Force left in 1966.

Nothing remains of the 1773 presidio U.S. troops occupied 1849-1851 except the chapel. It was rebuilt in 1877.

THE POST OF SAN ELIZARIO

Farm Road 258, 15 miles southeast of El Paso, El Paso County.

The Spanish established a presidio here in 1773 to protect the missions on the Rio Grande. It was part of the system devised by the Marques de Rubi to protect the settlements on the Rio Grande from Comanches. But the forts never afforded much protection from Comanches. The Indians simply avoided them. There was a Mexican garrison here after the Texas Revolution. U.S. troops were here briefly during the Mexican War and they returned in 1849. Troops were stationed here from then until 1851. It was an outpost of Fort Bliss.

Confederate troops occupied San Elizario in the early stages of the Civil War. But the area was under Union control from 1862 until the end of the war.

Fort Martin Scott
Fort Inge
Fort Croghan
Fort Graham
Fort Worth
Fort Lincoln
Fort Gates
Fort Merrill

THE FIRST LINE
OF FRONTIER FORTS

FORT MARTIN SCOTT

*U.S. 290, 2½ miles southeast
of Fredericksburg,
Gillespie County.*

The Army was establishing posts on the Indian frontier at the same time the forts on the border were being set up.

The first frontier fort was established December 5, 1848, outside the German town of Fredericksburg in Gillespie County. It was named Fort Martin Scott in honor of a major of the 5th Infantry, killed in 1847 at the Battle of Molino del Rey in Mexico.

The first garrison was composed of units of the 1st Infantry commanded by Captain Seth Eastman. The purpose was to protect the traffic on the road between Fredericksburg and San Antonio from the Comanches. There is no record of any battles being fought here. The frontier was moving rapidly westward and Fort Martin Scott was manned only occasionally after 1852. Confederate troops used it during the Civil War. Union troops did not return to it after the war.

FORT INGE

*Off Farm Road 140 about
2½ miles southeast of Uvalde,
Uvalde County.*

Troops of the 1st Infantry commanded by Captain Sidney Burbank established Fort Inge on March 13, 1849, as part of the frontier system. The site on the Leona River was chosen because the road to Eagle Pass branched off here from the road between San Antonio and El Paso.

The post was named for Lieutenant Zebulon Inge of the 2nd Dragoons, killed at Resaca de la Palma in 1846. The main business of the garrison was providing escorts

Top: A few foundation stones are still visible at the site once occupied by Fort Inge. Uvalde County maintains a park and campground here on the bank of the Leona River.

Opposite: The sites of the frontier forts and many other notable sites were marked with gray granite monuments like this during the Centennial celebration in 1936. Nothing is left of Fort Martin Scott.

for travelers. The troops stationed here had several encounters with hostile Indians.

Nothing very substantial ever was built at Fort Inge. There were only about a dozen buildings of log and timber construction. Robert E. Lee is said to have stopped at Fort Inge once, but he never was stationed here.

The troops left Fort Inge in April of 1851, returned in June of the same year, left again in 1855 and returned in 1856. The fort was abandoned to the Confederates in 1861 and reoccupied by U.S. troops only briefly after the war. It was abandoned permanently in 1869.

Several pioneer buildings have been moved to the site of old Fort Croghan to create a small museum. The state marker here recalls that the fort site was owned by pioneer settler Peter Kerr.

FORT CROGHAN

*Highway 29, west of
net, Burnet County.*

Units of the 2nd Dragoons comma Fort Croghan March 18, 1849, on Burnet. The post was first called to honor George Croghan. He w₂ and he died shortly afterward.

This post was on the Indian f moving westward pretty fast was abandoned in 1853.

Charles H. Tyler established Creek in the present city of e name was changed in 1850 vhen the post was established

tablished. But the frontier was state at the time. Fort Croghan

FORT GRAHAM

*Off Farm Road 2604, 5 miles
northwest of Whitney,
Hill County.*

Captain Ripley Arnold and units of the 2nd Dragoons established a post on the Brazos River in what is now Hill County on March 27, 1849. This camp was on the site of a former Indian camp, but the Indians were not troublesome here. The frontier soon moved farther west and this camp was abandoned in 1853.

The original name of this post was Camp Thornton. It was renamed, probably, for Lieutenant Colonel William Graham. He was one of the officers of the 11th Infantry killed at the Battle of Molino del Rey in Mexico in 1847. The last troops left November 9, 1853. The site never had been owned by the government. The buildings were used by cattle drivers and travelers. A settlement eventually grew up around the site but it didn't last. The Texas Centennial Commission built a replica of one of the barracks buildings and put up a marker at the site in 1936.

Nothing remains at the site of the original Fort Graham. Hill County built this small museum in the 1980s, using some of the stones that had been used to build a replica in the 1930s. The waters of Lake Whitney cut off access to the replica, on the original fort site. This little museum is about a half-mile away, on higher ground.

FORT WORTH

Courthouse Square, Belknap and Main, downtown Fort Worth, Tarrant County.

Captain Ripley Arnold and Company F of the 2nd Dragoons moved up from Fort Graham in the summer of 1849 and established a post near where the Clear Fork and the West Fork of the Trinity River meet. This post was originally on the lower river bank and it was called Camp Worth. The post was moved to the top of the bluff on the south side of the river because the first site was subject to flooding. The name was changed to Fort Worth in November of 1849.

The camp and fort were named for General William Jenkins Worth. He was commander of the Department of Texas when he died of cholera in San Antonio on May 7, 1849.

The government never owned the land under Fort Worth. Middleton T. Johnson and Archibald Robinson owned it and they let the Army use it, free. They were glad to have the troops in the neighborhood.

The Dragoons based at Fort Worth had an encounter with Comanches during the first year they were here. The Comanches came in from the west and apparently planned to attack the fort. A fur trader discovered them camped near the fort. He tipped off Major Arnold. The Dragoons attacked the Indians the same night. The Comanches fled. The soldiers chased them for two days and killed one of their chiefs.

Major Arnold and the Dragoons moved back to Fort Graham in 1851. Two

This bronze tablet, set in stone, commemorates the flimsy frontier fort that gave birth to the city of Fort Worth. The Tarrant County Courthouse complex occupies the site where the fort stood.

companies of the 8th infantry commanded by Captain J.V. Bomford occupied Fort Worth until Arnold and his Dragoons returned in January of 1852 to stay until August of the same year. They returned to Fort Graham then and Company B of the 2nd Dragoons under Major Hamilton Merrill occupied Fort Worth until it was abandoned in September of 1853. The frontier had moved. There were several federal forts west of Fort Worth by 1853.

Only log buildings were built here and settlers took them over after the army left. Nothing survives from that time. There is a marker on the southeast corner of the Tarrant County Criminal Courthouse grounds.

FORT LINCOLN

Lieutenant James Longstreet and a company of the 8th Infantry established a post 50 miles west of San Antonio on July 7, 1849. The site was on the road between San Antonio and Fort Duncan. The purpose was to provide escorts for travelers and protection for settlers. Comanches raided the stables at the fort at least once, in 1851. The settlers in the area were mostly Alsations developing the towns of Quihi, Castroville and D'Hanis in Henri Castro's colony. This post was just two miles from D'Hanis. There were 29 families living at D'Hanis at the time.

The post was named Fort Lincoln, for one of the officers of the 8th Infantry killed in the Mexican War. Captain George Lincoln fell at Buena Vista February 23, 1847.

Fort Lincoln was on a site Charles de Montel and a company of Texas Rangers had used as a base earlier. The fort had barracks for two companies of troops by 1851 and a hospital and quartermaster's warehouse. But the buildings were not very substantial. They were all wood and some of them had canvas roofs. The Army abandoned the post in July of 1852 because the frontier had moved. The Rangers used the buildings off and on for several years. *The Handbook of Texas* says the materials eventually were hauled off and re-used in buildings in D'Hanis.

FORT GATES

*Old Fort Gates Road, 2 miles
east of State Highway 36, South
of Gatesville, Coryell County.*

The federal frontier forts in Texas generally were open posts with buildings arranged around a parade ground and no real fortifications. Fort Gates was different. It was built inside a stockade.

This post was established October 26, 1849, by Captain William Montgomery and units of the 8th Infantry. The site was on the military road between Austin and Fort Graham. The main purpose of the fort was to protect settlers in the immediate vicinity.

There were four companies of Infantry here in 1850. The fort was on the north bank of the Leon River above Coryell Creek. It was named for Captain C.R. Gates. He was one of the heroes of the Mexican War and he had died shortly before this post was established.

There were 17 buildings at Fort Gates and an 18th was under construction when the army decided the post was no longer needed. The frontier had moved. The settlers here were no longer having problems with Indians. The garrison was withdrawn in March of 1852. Gates was the first frontier fort to outlive its usefulness. Only a few stone chimneys were standing a few years later.

Nothing is left of Fort Gates. A horse farm now occupies the site.

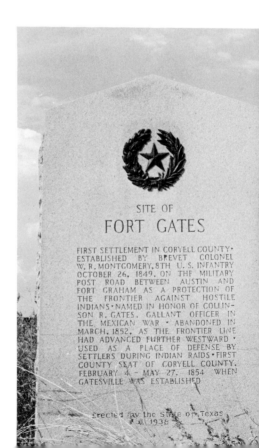

SITE OF
FORT GATES

FIRST SETTLEMENT IN CORYELL COUNTY·
ESTABLISHED BY BREVET COLONEL
W. R. MONTGOMERY, 8TH U. S. INFANTRY
OCTOBER 26, 1849, ON THE MILITARY
POST ROAD BETWEEN AUSTIN AND
FORT GRAHAM AS A PROTECTION OF
THE FRONTIER AGAINST HOSTILE
INDIANS·NAMED IN HONOR OF COLLIN-
SON R. GATES, GALLANT OFFICER IN
THE MEXICAN WAR · ABANDONED IN
MARCH, 1852, AS THE FRONTIER LINE
HAD ADVANCED FURTHER WESTWARD ·
USED AS A PLACE OF DEFENSE BY
SETTLERS DURING INDIAN RAIDS·FIRST
COUNTY SEAT OF CORYELL COUNTY,
FEBRUARY 4 - MAY 27, 1854 WHEN
GATESVILLE WAS ESTABLISHED

Erected by the State of Texas
1936

FORT MERRILL

*Off U.S. 281, 3½ miles
northwest of Dinero,
Live Oak County.*

Fort Merrill was established in March of 1850 to protect settlers and travelers on the road between San Antonio and Corpus Christi. The fort was on the right bank of the Nueces River, about 50 miles from Corpus Christi. The first troops stationed here were the men of Company H and Company K of the 1st Infantry, commanded by Captain S.M. Plummer. The troops themselves did most of the construction work. Some of the materials were shipped in from New Orleans. The buildings were made of lumber and logs.

Fort Merrill was named for Captain Hamilton Merrill of the 2nd Dragoons, or Captain Moses Merrill of the 5th Infantry, depending upon which account you prefer.

Fort Merrill was manned only intermittently after 1853 and it was abandoned in December of 1855.

Fort Belknap
Fort Mason
Fort Phantom Hill
Fort Terrett
Fort McKavett
Camp Johnson
Fort Ewell
Fort Clark
Fort Chadbourne
Fort Davis
Fort Lancaster
Camp Cooper
Camp Verde
Camp Colorado
Camp Wood
Camp Hudson
Fort Quitman
Fort Stockton

THE SECOND LINE
AND THE ROAD WEST

The border forts and the first line of frontier forts were in place by early 1850; a couple of thousand soldiers to cope with more than 25,000 Indians. Most of the soldiers were infantrymen. They could defend their posts if they were attacked. The Dragoons could come close to matching the Indians in mobility and they generally had greater firepower, but the Comanches almost always had the advantage. They learned to avoid direct confrontations. Their specialty was guerilla warfare — lightning raids and quick retreats. They just scattered if they were followed.

The Indians' horses could live off whatever forage there was. The Army's horses needed grain. So feed had to be carried on any long patrol. This meant wagons, and they were trouble. The hot, dry weather on the Texas frontier shrank the wooden wheels on the Army wagons. The rims would come loose. The teamsters often had to use makeshift shims to keep the rims tight. Sometimes they had to reheat and remount the rims in the field. The mounted patrols were encumbered to the point that the Comanches and their allies had little difficulty staying out of the Army's path.

The Indians had excellent communications with smoke and sound signals. But they were careless about posting sentries at night and there were several cases where soldiers and Rangers caught them asleep. The Army took Texas Ranger companies into temporary federal service from time to time to help guard the frontier.

The mounted soldiers and Rangers were most effective as escorts. The presence of a few well-armed horsemen discouraged Indian attacks on wagon trains and mail coaches, but didn't prevent them altogether. A trip across west Texas was a risky undertaking. But thousands of Americans were taking the risk. An energetic man named Henry Skillman started operating a courier service between San Antonio and El Paso in 1850. Skillman was born in New Jersey and raised in Kentucky. He came west to work as a teamster on the Santa Fe Trail. He was a guide for several U.S. Army units during the Mexican War. He knew the West well and he knew an opportunity when he saw one. Skillman went to Washington in 1851 and wangled a contract to carry the U.S. mail between San Antonio and Santa Fe by way of El Paso.

Skillman started his service in November of 1851 carrying the mail himself on horseback. He was then 37 years old. He was soon using coaches to carry mail and passengers. There had been coach service of sorts between Houston and San Antonio for several years. Most communities in the older parts of the state had some kind of coach service before 1850. But Henry Skillman was the pioneer operator in the West.

Settlers were moving west, too, in the early 1850s. The Army started a new line of forts.

FORT BELKNAP

State Highway 251, 2 miles south of Newcastle, Young County.

The first fort in the Army's second line of frontier posts was located originally about 10 miles above the junction of the Salt Fork and the Clear Fork of the Brazos River. The post was first called Camp Belknap. It became Fort Belknap and moved about two miles to get a better water supply. The recorded date of the first establishment was June 13, 1851. The move occurred in November of the same year.

Historian W.C. Holden says 10 companies of the 5th Infantry led by Colonel G. Loomis founded this post. There is another report that General William G. Belknap led the first garrison here, himself. The post was named for General Belknap and he was stationed here. He was transferred to Texas from Fort Gibson, Indian Territory, in May of 1851. *The Handbook of Texas* says he died in November of 1851, at

Two buildings have been restored and two have been rebuilt at old Fort Belknap. This is now a county park.

Fort Belknap. General Belknap was 57 and a veteran of the Mexican War.

The first buildings here were log and jacal. Jacal buildings were made of logs set in the ground vertically. The Spanish and the Mexicans were using this kind of construction before the Anglos came to Texas. There were not many trees in this part of Texas big enough for the horizontal log construction practiced by the Anglos in eastern Texas. There were two stone buildings at Fort Belknap by 1854 and several more by 1856. This was the biggest and busiest fort on the Texas frontier for several years before the Civil War.

Colonel Albert Sidney Johnston brought the U.S. 2nd Cavalry here in December of 1855. Johnston was soon ordered to the far west, himself, but units of the 2nd Cavalry remained on the Texas frontier until the beginning of the Civil War. Johnston and several other officers of the 2nd Cavalry joined the Confederacy when the war began. Some others stayed with the Union. Seventeen officers of this one regiment rose to the rank of general in one army or the other after 1861. Robert E. Lee was one of them. Some people suspected the secretary of war of using the 2nd Cavalry as a training ground for Southern officers. The secretary was Jefferson Davis.

The water supply was never very good at Fort Belknap. The Army abandoned the post in 1857 and moved the troops to Fort Griffin. A settlement had grown up around Fort Belknap. It was named Belknap and designated the county seat when Young County was organized in 1856. The settlement continued to thrive after the troops left. The Butterfield Overland Mail Line established a station in Belknap in 1858. Another stage line ran between Belknap and Dallas, through Fort Worth on a road that is still called Belknap Street today. Belknap was an important junction.

The buildings of Fort Belknap were occupied occasionally by troops of the Texas Frontier Regiment during the Civil War. Two hundred Comanche and Kiowa Indians

One of the rebuilt buildings at Fort Belknap houses a collection of pioneer artifacts and old military equipment.

came down from Indian Territory in the fall of 1864 and attacked one of the regiment's outposts near Belknap. They killed five troopers and four civilians in the Elm Creek settlement nearby. The Indians kidnapped eight people including Mrs. Brit Johnson and her two children.

Brit Johnson was a respected free black man. He won more respect by tracking down the kidnappers and persuading them to free his family and two of the other captives.

Fort Belknap was in very poor condition by the time federal troops returned in 1867. The new garrison was starting to make repairs when orders came to abandon

the post and move to Fort Griffin. The troops never returned. The government did not own the land and a settler filed a claim on it. A few of the buildings were rebuilt for the Centennial in 1936.

The city of Belknap declined after the county government moved to Graham in 1874. The fort site is now a county park.

Some white settlers held it against Robert Neighbors that he took his duties as Indian Agent seriously. He was gunned down in the street here at Belknap after he returned from escorting the Indians from the Brazos and Comanche reservations to Oklahoma in 1859.

FORT MASON

*South side of Mason,
Mason County.*

Two companies of the 2nd Dragoons commanded by Captain Hamilton Merrill established a post on a hill between San Saba and the Llano River on July 6, 1851, and named it for George T. Mason. He was a lieutenant in the Dragoons when he was killed by Mexicans in a skirmish near Fort Brown in 1846.

The Dragoons, themselves, built most of the original buildings with local timber and stone. There is a story that the second commanding officer at Fort Mason tricked the local Indian chiefs into thinking he had some very special magic. Lieutenant Colonel Charles May supposedly sent for the Indian leaders shortly after he arrived in the fall of 1851. He told them he was going to kill one of their dogs and bring it back to life. He chloroformed the animal and cut off a few small pieces of its tail to show the chiefs how dead it was. He "resurrected" the dog when the chloroform wore off. The Indians knew nothing about chloroform but they knew strong medicine when they saw it. They gave May and Fort Mason a lot of respect for a while.

The Dragoons were here until January of 1854. Fort Mason was abandoned then until March of 1855. It was occupied until May of 1855 and abandoned again.

The 2nd Cavalry arrived to reactivate Fort Mason in January of 1856. Secretary of War Jefferson Davis had established the 1st and 2nd Cavalry in 1855. He personally picked the officers. Albert Sidney Johnston was the commanding officer of the 2nd Cavalry. Robert E. Lee was second in command in 1856. Lee later commanded the 2nd Cavalry units in Texas and was commanding officer of Fort Mason on two occasions.

The men of the 2nd Cavalry wore rakish hats no other soldiers were permitted to wear. They were mounted on the best Kentucky horses the Army could afford. The horses were assigned to the various companies by color. Company A had all greys; B and E had sorrels; C, D and F had bays; G and H had browns. Company K had all roan horses. No outfit in the Army had more class or more great names. John Bell Hood was one of the lieutenants. He led Company G on a patrol out of Fort Mason in 1857 that covered 500 miles and eliminated 19 Indians. Hood was an able and popular officer. He rose to rank of lieutenant general in the Confederate Army during the Civil War.

One of the captains in the 2nd Cavalry was Charles Travis. It may have been because of his name that he was chosen for a commission in this select regiment.

Fort Mason occupied this site on a hill south of the present town of Mason. No soldiers ever occupied this building. It is a replica built a long time after the settlers had borrowed the last stones from the original buildings.

Charles had no military background. But he had been a captain in the Texas Rangers and he was the only son of the Alamo hero, William Barret Travis. Charles didn't last long in the 2nd Cavalry. One of the other officers accused him of libel and slander. The complaint had something to do with a gambling debt and there is evidence that the officers of this outfit were a pretty touchy bunch. Anyway, Charles Travis was tried by a court-martial and found guilty of conduct unbecoming an officer. He was dismissed from the Army in May, 1856.

Top: The only son of the Alamo hero William Barret Travis served with the 2nd Cavalry at Fort Mason. Charles Travis was seven when his father was killed at the Alamo. He was a member of the legislature and a member of the Texas Rangers before he was appointed a captain in the cavalry in 1855. Charles was dismissed in 1856 after a court martial found him guilty conduct unbecoming an officer.

Opposite: Lieutenant Colonel Charles May used chloroform in a trick to make the Indians think he had magic powers when he was commanding officer at Fort Mason in 1851.

A committee of the Texas legislature branded the charge unfounded and the verdict unfair. The legislature asked President James Buchanan to pardon Travis. But the conviction still stood when Travis died of tuberculosis at Chappell Hill in 1860 at the age of 31.

Lieutenant Colonel Robert E. Lee was in command at Fort Mason in January of 1861 when secession fever was nearing the boiling point. He wrote a letter from here saying he could anticipate no greater calamity for the country than dissolution of the Union.

There had been a few Indian raids in the vicinity of Fort Mason in 1860, but the two years before that had been fairly quiet. There were no Confederate or state forces here regularly during the Civil War. The Indians grew much bolder, killing and kidnapping settlers. There was even less protection immediately after the war and the Indians took full advantage of the situation. The frontier was also infested with outlaws, draft dodgers and rustlers. Federal troops began returning to Fort Mason in 1866. There were 500 men of the 4th Cavalry here by January of 1867. They lived in tents. The buildings were in ruins. The Union troops had set fire to them when they left in 1861 and the settlers hauled off a lot of the stones after that.

The cavalrymen started to rebuild the fort but they were transferred in April of 1868. A company of the 35th Infantry moved in but stayed less than a year. The fort was abandoned for the last time in January of 1869.

The government had never owned the land and it went back to private ownership. All the original buildings are gone.

More than a dozen officers stationed at Fort Mason with the 2nd Cavalry in the late 1850s won fame during the Civil War. John Bell Hood was a lieutenant in the U.S. Army when he was here. He joined the Confederate army in 1861 and rose to the rank of Lieutenant General. Hood's Texas Brigade, Hood County and Fort Hood were named for John Bell Hood.

FORT PHANTOM HILL

Farm Road 600, 14 miles north of Abilene, Jones County.

Colonel J.J. Abercrombie and two companies of the 5th Infantry established this post on November 14, 1851. The Army never called it Phantom Hill. It was not even designated a fort. The Army's name for it was Post on the Clear Fork of the Brazos.

The soldiers built most of the buildings themselves. The materials were lumber and logs. The chimneys were built with the local limestone. The soldiers stationed here escorted travelers and the wagon trains hauling supplies from Austin. They made frequent patrols, too, looking for Indians. The duty was monotonous and morale was low. Soldiers often deserted. Duty at this post was considered especially undesirable. The water supply was unreliable. The vegetable garden was not productive. The weather was disagreeable and the Indians were dangerous.

The garrison was transferred in April of 1854. One of the soldiers set fire to the

Top: This fort is a national historic landmark. The ruins are right on Farm Road 600 and the property owners are very tolerant of sightseers and photographers.

Opposite: This sketch of Fort Phantom Hill in the National Archives must have been done in the early 1850s. The buildings were burned when the troops left here in 1854.

buildings as he left. This supposedly was to make sure the garrison would never have to return to the post.

The Army did not occupy the post again on a regular basis. But it did serve occasionally as an outpost of Fort Griffin after the Civil War. The Butterfield Overland Mail Line had a station here in 1858. The station was surrounded by the stone chimneys of the burned buildings. The scene looked ghostly on moonlit nights. It was probably about this time that it began to be called Phantom Hill.

There is a legend that Robert E. Lee was commander here once. This probably is not true, but he may well have been here occasionally. He was stationed nearby at Fort Mason and at Camp Cooper at different times.

What is left of Fort Phantom hill is on private property.

The limestone chimneys orphaned when
the fort buildings were burned more than a
hundred years ago make a spooky scene.
They're the reason settlers and travelers
started calling this Phantom Hill. The Army
never called it that.

FORT TERRETT

Just north of I-10 on an un-numbered county road at the eastern edge of Sutton County.

Units of the 1st Infantry led by Lieutenant Colonel Henry Bainbridge established this post on February 2, 1852. The site they chose was on the east bank of the North Llano River.

The post was originally called Post on the Rio Llano. The name was changed to Fort Terrett October 6, 1852. Lieutenant John Terrett was one of the officers of the 1st Infantry killed at the Battle of Monterrey in 1846.

Top: The Noels' ranch house is built around two of the original officers' quarters. The commanding officer's house and the stone commissary warehouse are still standing, too.

Opposite: William Noel's Fort Terrett Ranch occupies the site where the Army built an infantry post in 1852.

The soldiers did most of the building at Fort Terrett. They used stone. There wasn't much timber. There were 250 men stationed here at one time. The post was on the road between San Antonio and El Paso so there was plenty of traffic to be protected. But Fort McKavett was just 30 miles away. The War Department decided in 1854 that both forts were not needed. Fort Terrett was abandoned on February 26, 1854.

The troops didn't stay here long. They were gone by 1854.

SITE OF

FORT TERRETT

ESTABLISHED FEBRUARY 5, 1852 BY
THE UNITED STATES ARMY AS A
PROTECTION TO FRONTIER SETTLERS ·
NAMED IN HONOR OF LIEUTENANT
JOHN C. TERRETT WHO FELL AT
MONTERREY, SEPTEMBER 21, 1846 ·
ABANDONED FEBRUARY 26, 1854

Erected by the State of Texas
1936

FORT McKAVETT

Junction of Farm Road 864 and Farm Road 1674, western Menard County.

This was another infantry post, named for an infantry officer. The post was established on March 14 of 1852. It was first called Camp San Saba and then Camp McKavett before it was named Fort McKavett.

The first troops stationed here were units of the 8th Infantry commanded by Major Edmund Alexander. The fort was named for Captain Henry McKavett. He was with the 8th Infantry in Mexico when he was killed at the Battle of Monterrey on September 21, 1846. The original buildings were stone and the soldiers built most of them.

This post was near the road between San Antonio and El Paso and only 21 miles from the ruins of an old presidio the Spanish had built in the 1750s to protect a mission that turned out to be not very successful. The Comanches drove the missionaries away in 1758. There was a persistent legend that the Spanish had discovered gold and silver near the San Saba de la Santa Cruz Mission. The story was that they had

This photograph may have been made after the troops left and settlers moved into the stone buildings in the middle 1880s.

left a lot of refined silver in a cave. There've been treasure hunters looking for it almost ever since. Some people believed that Jim Bowie had discovered the Spanish silver before he was killed at the Alamo. He never told anybody else where it was, if he did.

Units of the 8th and 2nd Infantry and units of the 2nd Dragoons were stationed here at different times before the Civil War. Albert Sidney Johnston was here in 1855 when he learned that Jefferson Davis had chosen him to command the new 2nd United States Cavalry. Fort McKavett was abandoned in 1859. The buildings were

falling down by the time federal troops returned to the frontier after the Civil War.

This post was not reoccupied until 1869. Units of the 4th Cavalry were stationed here then. Colonel Ranald Mackenzie was in command. Mackenzie was an outstanding soldier and a good housekeeper. He put his troops to work restoring the post and it was one the few frontier forts where the post surgeon actually approved of the living conditions and sanitary measures. There were barracks for eight companies here by 1876 and stone houses for the officers, stables and a stone hospital building.

At least one officer thought it was an extravagance to build permanent buildings at the frontier forts. J. Evetts Haley quotes the quartermaster general at Fort

Top: Fort McKavett is a state park. There are no provisions for camping, but there is no admission fee, either. The building in the background was the post hospital. It is now a museum.

Opposite: The ruin in the left foreground is what is left of the commanding officer's house. It burned in the 1930s, 50 years after the Army abandoned Fort McKavett. *Inset:* The father of baseball once lived in this house. Abner Doubleday was once commanding officer here.

Concho as arguing in 1868 that the stone walls and chimneys of abandoned posts like Belknap and Phantom Hill were monuments to waste. He thought temporary buildings were sufficient on a frontier that plainly was moving. But the construction of permanent buildings continued and there were several instances where construction was going on right up until the time a fort was abandoned.

Fort McKavett was abandoned in 1883. But some of the stone buildings are still standing. The government never owned the land. It reverted to private ownership when the soldiers left. The buildings were occupied by settlers. The old fort became a little town. The property was divided and pieces were sold off over the years. Eventually, the owner of one of the tracts gave his property to the state for a park. The Parks and Wildlife Department then started buying up the other tracts and restoring some of the buildings. What is left of the old fort is now a state park.

CAMP JOHNSTON

South bank of North Concho River, northwestern Tom Green County.

The 8th Infantry set up an outpost in March of 1852 on the North Concho River. There were five companies stationed here, but it never became a permanent post. The troops moved on to what became Fort Chadbourne in the fall of 1852.

The Handbook of Texas says this outpost was named for Joseph E. Johnston. He was the army's chief topographical engineer in Texas at the time. He later commanded the Army of Tennessee in the Civil War. Johnston conducted the survey of the boundary between Texas and New Mexico.

There were no permanent buildings and nothing remains.

The Parks and Wildlife Department is rebuilding some of Fort McKavett's ruined buildings, but some will be left in ruins.

FORT EWELL

*Farm Road 468, 25 miles
southeast of Cotulla,
LaSalle County.*

Lieutenant Colonel William Loring and troops of the Mounted Rifles established this post on May 18, 1852, on the Nueces River. The post was on the road between San Antonio and Laredo. It was named for Captain Richard Ewell of the 1st Dragoons. He was a veteran of the war in Mexico.

The buildings at Fort Ewell were adobe and they did not survive. The fort was abandoned on October 3, 1854, and the troops were transferred to Fort McIntosh. There was no longer any need for a fort here and the garrison surely was glad to go somewhere else. The site was surrounded by marshes and infested with mosquitos. One of the Army's inspectors reported in 1853 that a less inviting spot could not be conceived.

A settlement had grown up around the little fort. It survived for a time after the soldiers left. The settlement was called LaSalle and it was the county seat of LaSalle County for a short time after the county was organized in 1880. The site is private property. The Army never owned it.

Most of the buildings at Fort Clark are in good shape and many people live here. But the old commissary warehouse is being neglected. This was an active base until the end of World War II.

FORT CLARK

U.S. 90, Brackettville,
Kinney County.

This base was called Fort Riley when it was established on June 19, 1852, by Captain Joseph LaMotte and two companies of the 1st Infantry.

The name was changed to Fort Clark July 15, 1852, in honor of Major John B. Clark of the 1st Infantry. He was one of the officers killed in the Mexican War.

This was an obvious site for a fort in 1852. It was on the road between San Antonio and El Paso. It was on one of the branches of the war trail the Comanches followed on their raids into Mexico and it was at the southern end of the line of frontier forts as it existed at that time. The fort was established at Las Moras Spring. This ensured

General Jonathan Wainwright was in command at Fort Clark until shortly before Pearl Harbor. He went from here to the Philippines. Wainwright surrendered the American forces in the Philippines to the Japanese after General Douglas MacArthur withdrew to Australia.

a supply of good water for the post and denied the Comanches one of their major watering holes. Fort Clark was a stop on the San Antonio-El Paso Mail Line from the beginning. The Butterfield Overland never came this way.

The government eventually bought the land Fort Clark was built on but it was rented, in the beginning, from Sam Maverick of San Antonio.

The fort was laid out around a big parade ground on a limestone ridge above the spring. Temporary buildings gradually were replaced by stone barracks buildings and nine stone houses for the officers. The commissary and the hospital were also built of stone.

Confederates occupied Fort Clark only briefly after the U.S. troops left in 1861. The U.S. troops returned to the fort in 1866. The first troops here after the war were units of the 4th Cavalry led by Captain John Wilcox. John Bullis and his Seminole Indian Scouts achieved much of their fame while stationed here. They went along when Colonel Ranald Mackenzie and the 4th Cavalry rode into Mexico in 1873 to break up the camps of the Kickapoo and Lipan Apache Indians blamed for a series

of raids on the Texas side of the Rio Grande. The relentless Mackenzie kept his troopers in the saddle for four days and nights without sleep on the foray.

The Army started adding new buildings here in the late 1860s and by the 1870s this was a major post. The officers and their wives had a busy social schedule. There was a dance every weekend. They were calling them hops then. There was a farewell party every time an officer was transferred and a welcoming party every time a new officer arrived. But it wasn't all fun and games. The women complained a lot about the heat and the insects and the Army's method of assigning quarters was very disruptive. An officer arriving for duty at a fort was entitled to claim any quarters he chose if they were occupied by an officer of lesser rank. A major could cause a

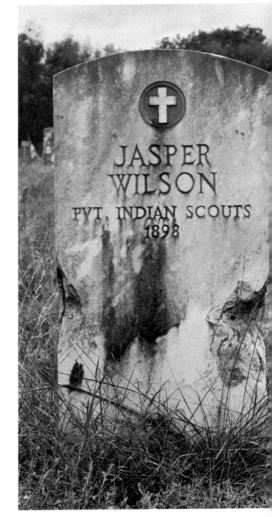

Some of the Army's redoubtable Seminole Indian scouts are buried in a little cemetery just outside Fort Clark. The scouts were descended from Negro slaves and Seminole Indians. They were experts at tracking Indian war parties. Fort Clark was their main base in the 1870s.

Opposite: The oldest building at Fort Clark is this jacal hut built before the Civil War. Lieutenant Colonel Robert E. Lee is said to have been a member of a court-martial panel that once sat in this building.

whole series of moves because the officer he put out could claim the quarters of any officer he out-ranked, and that officer could do the same thing, on down the line.

General William T. Sherman came here in 1882 on a tour of the border forts. He said Fort Clark was the biggest and most expensive fort in Texas. He suggested it ought to be closed, but his recommendation was not followed.

The 3rd Texas Volunteer Infantry came here in 1899 to hold the fort while the regular garrison went to Cuba to fight the Spanish. The 5th Cavalry was based here from 1920 to 1940. Robert E. Lee, William Shafter, Phillip Sheridan, John Bankhead Magruder and George Patton all spent some time at Fort Clark. General Jonathan Wainwright was the commanding officer here in 1939 shortly before he went to the Philippines, where he was captured by the Japanese. Wainwright made a hit with the troops by building the big swimming pool that is still in use on the site.

Few soldiers use the Fort Clark swimming pool today. The Army sold the property in 1946. It is now a condominium resort.

The walls of the barracks are still standing at old Fort Chadbourne. The ruins are not visible from the highway. The site is on a ranch owned by a banker in Ballinger.

FORT CHADBOURNE

*Off U.S. 277, 10 miles north of
Bronte, Coke County.*

Units of the 8th Infantry led by Captain John Beardsley established Fort
Chadbourne October 28, 1852. The post was originally called Camp on Oak Creek.
The name was changed, first to Camp Chadbourne and then to Fort Chadbourne.
This name was chosen to honor Lieutenant Theodore Chadbourne. He was serving
with the 8th Infantry when he was killed at Resaca de la Palma on May 9, 1846.
Chadbourne was one of the first casualties of the Mexican War.

Fort Chadbourne was situated on the east side of Oak Creek about 13 miles above
its junction with the Colorado River. There were three stone buildings: two barracks
and the hospital. The officers' houses were jacal. The water supply never was very
good at Fort Chadbourne and the Army abandoned the post in 1859. The Butterfield
Overland Mail Line had established a station at the fort in 1858. Butterfield Overland
coaches continued to use the station until the Civil War shut the service down in 1861.

The last Butterfield Overland eastbound coach came through here in March of
1861. Texas secessionists detained the coach to make sure Horace Greely was not

on board. The famous publisher had been in California preaching abolition to the already converted. He had said he was going to return to the East Coast on the Butterfield Overland. But he took a steamer, instead. The stagecoach was allowed to proceed when the Texans were satisfied Greely was not on board.

Federal troops returned to Fort Chadbourne in 1867 and started to repair the buildings. But the water supply had not improved. The troops left in December of the same year to establish a new post at what became Fort Concho. The San Antonio-El Paso Stage Line used Chadbourne as a station for a time after the troops left.

Settlers occupied the buildings and the old fort was a town for a few years. The site is private property and the stone buildings are ruins.

FORT DAVIS

State Highway 17, in
Fort Davis, Jeff Davis County.

Travelers crossing Texas on the way to California came through what are now called the Davis Mountains almost from the time travel to California started. Lieutenant William Whiting explored this route for the U.S. Army in 1849. The route followed a creekbed a good part of the way through the mountains. Some accounts say Lieutenant Whiting named this stream Limpia Creek. But it is a Spanish name, so it probably goes farther back. The mountains then were called the Limpia Mountains.

Major Jefferson Van Horne brought his troops through the Limpia Canyon on his way out to establish the post that became Fort Bliss. Henry Skillman was running

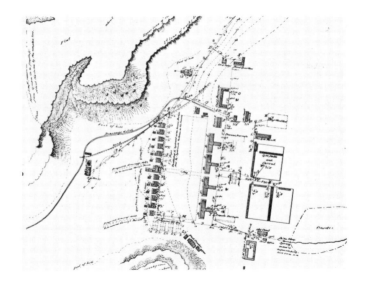

Army engineers drew this plan of Fort Davis when they were planning a water distribution system in the 1880s. The fort had already outlived its usefulness but people were not quite sure yet that the Indian wars were over in Texas.

stage coaches through the canyon by the early 1850s. He had a stage station here. But the concept of stations with corrals and fresh teams of mules was not developed until later. Skillman's coaches made overnight stops on the road, camping out. This was risky business. There were Apaches living in the Limpia Mountains and Comanches often passed through. Skillman's crews counted on holding the Indians off with the new Sharps .52 caliber carbines Skillman had brought back from the East. Sometimes they did and sometimes they died in the attempt. Skillman was carrying military mail so some of the western post commanders joined him in urging more protection for the road.

General Persifor Smith was commander of the Department of Texas in 1854. He made a personal inspection of the area and authorized establishment of an Army post in the Limpia Canyon. Lieutenant Colonel Washington Seawell and six companies of the 8th Infantry arrived October 7, 1854, and picked a site in a canyon near the headwaters of Limpia Creek. The land was claimed about the same time by John James under a bounty warrant he had bought. The Army negotiated a lease and agreed to pay James $300 a year.

The camp was named for Secretary of War Jefferson Davis. Most of the original buildings were timber. The Butterfield Overland Mail Line established a station here in 1859 after the Post Office Department changed the line's original route.

The first troops got into a skirmish with Apaches on the way here and problems with Apaches continued until 1880. The Indians often attacked the mail coaches and travelers. Escorts and passengers were killed with some frequency. There is a story that in one attack in 1859 the Indians killed the guard and stole the mail from one of the coaches on the road here. The Indians supposedly were gathered around looking at the illustrations in the newspapers and magazines they found in the mail

All of the buildings standing on officers' row in the 1880s diagram are standing today and they will be here for a long time.

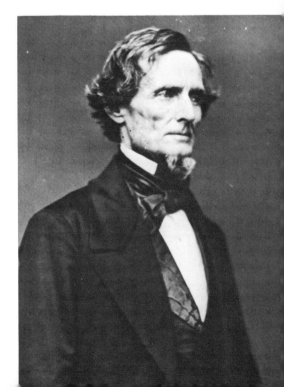

Top: The stone and adobe buildings here were falling down when the National Park Service took over the site in the 1960s and began restoring some of the buildings. Fort Davis is maintained now as a National Historic Site.

Right: This fort and the town adjacent to it, the mountains and the county all were named for Jefferson Davis. He was President Franklin Pierce's secretary of war when this base was established.

sacks when troops from Fort Davis surprised and killed 14 of them. This experience was said to have convinced the Apaches that magazine illustrations were bad medicine, to be avoided.

The Army Signal Corps started at Fort Davis. Army doctor Albert Myer was interested in sign language as a way to help deaf-mutes communicate. This caused him to pay more attention to the Indian's methods of signaling each other than he might otherwise have paid when he was stationed here. Myer started experimenting with a signal system. The Army adopted it in 1858. Dr. Myer became the Army's first signal officer in 1860.

Texas Confederate cavalrymen moved into Fort Davis when the Union troops left in 1861. The Apaches made a raid on a ranch near the fort in the summer of 1861. Lieutenant Reuben Mays took 14 men out to look for the Apaches. The Indians ambushed the Confederates and killed them all. Most settlers cleared out. There were no travelers to be protected and the Confederates abandoned Fort Davis after General H.H. Sibley's effort to capture New Mexico for the Confederacy failed in 1862. Union troops held the El Paso area after that and they reoccupied Fort Davis just long enough to show the flag. There was no reason to stay and they didn't. The Indians burned the abandoned buildings in 1863 and had things their way until after the end of the Civil War. They did not welcome the return of the federal troops in 1867.

Lieutenant Colonel Wesley Merritt was the first commander after the war. His garrison was made up of units of the 9th Cavalry and the 24th Infantry. The army hired 200 civilian carpenters and masons to rebuild the post. The materials this time were stone and adobe. The rent went up to $900 a year.

Mail coaches were back on the road between El Paso and San Antonio before the troops returned to Fort Davis. The losses the operators sufferd convinced the government the forts had to be re-established. The Apaches and Comanches were beginning to realize that the whites would not be satisfied just to *cross* their territories. They began to see that they were going to be displaced. They may have seen it before some of the whites. Colonel William Shafter, for instance, thought there never would be any settlers in this part of Texas. He was commanding officer

OVERLAND TRAIL
← EL PASO 200 MILES
SAN ANTONIO 380 MILES →

at Fort Davis in 1871 when he said the only reason for the fort was to protect the El Paso Mail Line.

Colonel Benjamin Grierson thought there certainly would be settlers and he wanted to be one of them. Grierson came to Fort Davis in 1880 with the 10th Cavalry to make war on the Apache band led by Chief Victorio. But it was in Mexico that the Apaches were finally cornered by Mexican troops in the fall of 1880. Victorio and most of his braves were killed. The last Indian raid in this part of Texas occurred in 1882. Colonel Grierson retired from the Army in 1890 after 22 years as commanding officer of the 10th Cavalry. He built a house near Fort Davis and lived here until he died in 1911. The fort was abandoned in 1891.

Top: Men of the 3rd Cavalry at Fort Davis, 1870s.

Opposite: Some of the federal forts were built to protect settlers. Fort Davis was built to protect travelers. The San Antonio-El Paso Mail Line and the Overland Mail Line both came through here. Settlers eventually came too.

FORT LANCASTER

*U.S. 290, 10 miles east of
Sheffield, Crockett County.*

The country around Fort Lancaster has not changed much since the fort was established here on August 20, 1855. It is still unpopulated semi-desert.

The site is on Live Oak Creek about a half-mile from the creek's junction with the Pecos River. It was established to give travelers on the road between San Antonio and El Paso more protection from the Indians. The first troops here were units of the 1st Infantry. The first commanding officer was Captain Stephen Carpenter. The post was originally called Camp Lancaster. It was designated a fort in 1856.

Colonel Joseph Mansfield came out to tour the western frontier in 1852. He met stagecoach operator Henry Skillman and traveled the road from El Paso to San Antonio with him. The colonel thought the road deserved more protection than it had been getting. He recommended reactivation of the post at El Paso. He also recommended new posts on the Rio Grande south of El Paso (Fort Quitman) and on Live Oak Creek just above the Pecos River. Fort Lancaster occupies the site the colonel suggested on Live Oak Creek.

The original buildings here were what the Army called hackadales. These were wood frames with canvas sides and roofs. They gradually were replaced by stone buildings arranged around an open parade ground in the usual frontier fashion.

There is a story that the troops here played a trick on the Apaches after the Indians attacked a small wagon train near the fort in 1857. The soldiers concealed themselves inside a couple of covered wagons and set out on the road to see if the Indians would

The site for Fort Lancaster was not chosen for its beauty. The fort was built to protect travelers on a dangerous and exposed stretch of desert.

attack them. The Indians did and 40 soldiers threw the canvas covers off their wagons and started shooting. The Apaches departed in haste.

The federal troops abandoned Fort Lancaster at the start of the Civil War and the fort never was really active again. It was used occasionally as an outpost. There is one report that troopers of the 9th Cavalry fought off an attack by an estimated 900 Indians, Mexicans and white renegades here in 1867. The buildings were not repaired after the war. The government never had owned the land. Only a few chimneys and fragments of walls are standing.

No town grew up around Fort Lancaster. Nobody wanted to live here. Crockett County gave the site to the Texas Parks and Wildlife Department in 1968 and it is open to visitors, free.

CAMP COOPER

17 miles south of Throckmorton off Ranch Road 2528, west of U.S. 283, Throckmorton County.

The Comanche Indians were the main reason the U.S. Army had to maintain so many forts on the Texas frontier. Secretary of War Jefferson Davis suggested to Governor Elisha Pease that Texas should put the Indians on reservations. The governor and the legislature accepted this suggestion and set aside more than 50,000 acres of land for the Indians in 1854. The state invited the federal government to locate the sites and maintain the reservations. Texas Indian Agent Robert Neighbors and Captain Randolph Marcy of the U.S. Army surveyed the frontier and chose the locations.

The Brazos Indian Reservation was located on the Brazos River 12 miles south of Fort Belknap in what is now Young County. The Comanche Indian Reserve was located on the Clear Fork of the Brazos in what is now Throckmorton County. Neighbors persuaded remnants of the Waco, Wichita, Anadarko, Caddo and Tonkawa tribes to settle on the Brazos Reservation. A few hundred Comanches under Chief Ketumse settled on the Comanche Reservation in 1855.

Colonel Albert Sidney Johnston was ordered to set up an Army post to prevent clashes between the Comanches and the white settlers. The colonel established the

Robert E. Lee was one of the most promising officers in the U.S. Army in 1855. That's why Jefferson Davis chose him to help lead the 2nd Cavalry Regiment established that year. Lee was a Lieutenant Colonel when he came here from the commandant's post at West Point to take command of Camp Cooper.

post on the bank of the Clear Fork on January 3, 1856. He stationed three companies of his 2nd Cavalry here.

Lieutenant Colonel Robert E. Lee arrived three months later to take over command of the post. Lee had just finished two years of duty as Superintendent of the U.S. Military Academy. The garrison was still living in tents when Lee arrived. These were gradually replaced with wood and canvas buildings. Lee was at Camp Cooper until July of 1857. He led several patrols out of here.

The reservations did not solve the Indian problem. The Comanches on the reservation were members of the Southern, or Penateka, band. They tried to learn

Camp Cooper was established to protect the settlers and the Indians on the Comanche Reservation from the hostile Comanches and Kiowas. There is a marker at the site but nothing is left of the post.

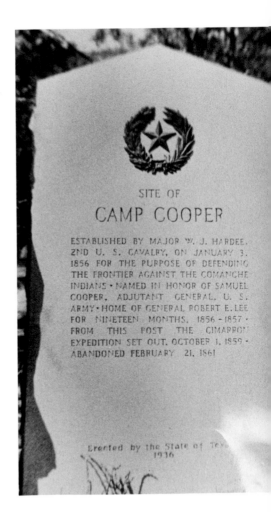

SITE OF

CAMP COOPER

ESTABLISHED BY MAJOR W. J. HARDEE, 2ND U. S. CAVALRY, ON JANUARY 3, 1856 FOR THE PURPOSE OF DEFENDING THE FRONTIER AGAINST THE COMANCHE INDIANS • NAMED IN HONOR OF SAMUEL COOPER, ADJUTANT GENERAL, U. S. ARMY • HOME OF GENERAL ROBERT E. LEE FOR NINETEEN MONTHS, 1856 - 1857 • FROM THIS POST THE CIMARRON EXPEDITION SET OUT, OCTOBER 1, 1859 • ABANDONED FEBRUARY 21, 1861

Erected by the State of Texas
1936

something about farming, but the weather was against them. Their crops didn't do well. Some left and returned to their former nomadic life. The tougher Quahadi Comanches never agreed to live on the reservation. They continued to raid farms and ranches and the reservation Indians got blamed for some of their mischief. There also were some provocations by whites determined to be rid of all Indians. Eight Indian braves from the Brazos Reservation were out on an authorized hunting expedition in December of 1858 when a party of whites attacked and killed them all. Another group of whites invaded the reservation in May of 1859 and killed two Indians. This caused a fight that left two whites and an Indian chief dead.

Major Neighbors gave up. He personally escorted the Indians to the Oklahoma Territory in August of 1859. Neighbors was shot to death at Fort Belknap September 14, shortly after he returned to Texas. His efforts to defend and protect the Indians had been deeply resented.

There was little need for Camp Cooper with the Indians gone. But some troops remained until the beginning of the Civil War.

Camp Cooper was named for Colonel Samuel Cooper. He was Adjutant General of the Army when the camp was established. The site was never owned by the government and it is private property still.

The Comanche Reservation was not a success. The Indians were moved to Oklahoma in 1859.

SITE OF THE PRINCIPAL
VILLAGE OF THE

COMANCHE INDIAN
RESERVE

ESTABLISHED IN 1854 · HERE COLONEL
ROBERT E. LEE, U. S. A., THEN COM -
MANDING CAMP COOPER, HELD A
PEACE PARLEY WITH CHIEF CATUMSEH
ON APRIL 11, 1856

Erected by the State of Texas
1936

CAMP VERDE

Off State Highway 173, 12 miles south of Kerrville, directly west of Camp Verde General Store.

Camp Verde had a unique history. The only camel corps the U.S. Army ever had was based here. This was a cavalry camp when it was established on the bank of Verde Creek in southern Kerr County in July of 1855, but the camels were coming.

Secretary of War Jefferson Davis had persuaded Congress in March of 1855 to give his department $30,000 for an experiment with camels. Davis' agents were in Africa shopping for camels when Camp Verde was established. An Army transport arrived at Indianola April 29, 1856, with 34 camels and five camel drivers. They reached Camp Verde in June. Secretary Davis wanted to know whether the camels would be better pack animals than the mules the Army was accustomed to using. So the Camp Verde garrison organized several prolonged expeditions into remote areas like the Big Bend. One caravan went all the way to California. The Army bought 41 more camels in 1857.

The camels passed every test. There had been some concern that their feet couldn't stand all the rocks. But the rocks were not a problem. The camels could carry much heavier loads than the mules and they needed less food and water. Some reports said the camels carried water for the horses and mules on some expeditions while going without water themselves for up to five days at a time. The experiment was a success. The Army built a big camel barn at Camp Verde and camels might have become commonplace on the frontier had not the Civil War intervened.

Eighty camels joined the Confederacy in February of 1861. Some of them were just turned loose. Some carried cotton to Mexico during the Union blockade.

A few camels were still in the neighborhood when federal troops returned to Camp Verde in 1866. They were sold when the Army abandoned the camp in 1869.

The only camel base the Army ever had is now a private ranch. The gate is just off State Highway 173, south of Kerrville.

Top: The camels based here were often on the road because Secretary Jefferson Davis wanted to know whether they were more practical than mules in the western desert. This camel was photographed at Camp Drum in Arizona.

The present owners of Camp Verde have turned the surviving officers' quarters into a comfortable ranch house.

CAMP COLORADO

Off State Highway 206, 14 miles northeast of Coleman, Coleman County.

Units of the 2nd Cavalry established this post originally in 1855 in what is now Mills County. Major Earl Van Dorn was in command when the post was moved to a site on Mukewater Creek, in what is now Coleman County, in August of 1856. It was moved again in July of 1857 to a site 20 miles north of Jim Ned Creek and here it remained until the Civil War. *The Handbook of Texas* says all the garrison except one lieutenant joined the Confederacy.

State Ranger units occupied the post part of the time during the Civil War. Federal troops never returned after the war.

The site is privately owned. The Texas Centennial Commission built a replica of the post administration building in the Coleman City Park in 1936.

Top: Nothing is left of Camp Colorado at the original site outside Coleman. It is private property.

Bottom: But a replica of the camp administration building survives in the Coleman City Park. The Texas Centennial Commission built the replica in 1936.

CAMP WOOD

*Junction of State Highway 55
and Farm Road 337, Real County.*

The Army had dropped the custom of naming frontier forts for officers killed in the Mexican War by the time Camp Wood was established on the Nueces River in May of 1857.

The camp was established by Captain J.B. Wood and a company of the 1st Cavalry. They named it for Captain Wood.

Camp Wood was 50 miles northwest of Fort Inge, very near the site of a mission the Spanish had established in 1762. The Mission San Lorenzo de la Santa Cruz was abandoned by 1768. The soldiers used some of the materials from the ruins to build shelters at Camp Wood. No permanent buildings were built. The troops left in March of 1861 as the Civil War began. The camp never was manned again after the war.

The town of Camp Wood is on the approximate site of the post.

The marker the Texas Centennial Commission put up at the site of Camp Wood in 1936 is immediately south of the present town of Camp Wood, on State Highway 55.

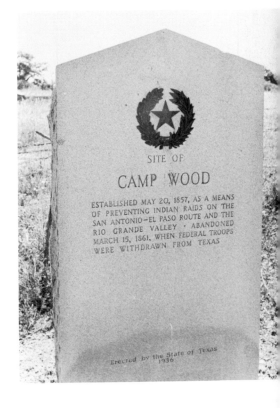

SITE OF

CAMP WOOD

ESTABLISHED MAY 20, 1857, AS A MEANS
OF PREVENTING INDIAN RAIDS ON THE
SAN ANTONIO—EL PASO ROUTE AND THE
RIO GRANDE VALLEY · ABANDONED
MARCH 15, 1861, WHEN FEDERAL TROOPS
WERE WITHDRAWN FROM TEXAS

Erected by the State of Texas
1936

CAMP HUDSON

*State Highway 163, 21 miles
north of Comstock,
Val Verde County.*

One account says this post was established in 1854. *The Handbook of Texas* gives the date as June 7, 1857. It was another link in the chain of posts protecting the road between San Antonio and El Paso.

Camp Hudson was situated on San Pedro Creek. This is a tributary of Devil's River in Val Verde County.

Camp Hudson was named for Lieutenant Walter Hudson after he died of wounds he received in a fight with Indians. The troops stationed here had some encounters with Comanches and followed them into Mexico a couple of times. One of the experimental camel caravans from Camp Verde came through here in 1859. The officer in charge said he was impressed by the patience and endurance of the animals. The federal troops left in 1861. They returned in 1868 and left for good in January of 1877. The government never owned the real estate.

There is a state marker on Highway 163 north of Comstock. The camp site is on private property. There are no buildings standing.

Nothing is left where Fort Quitman was except a tiny cemetery.

FORT QUITMAN

5½ miles southeast of Esperanza, Farm Road 192, Hudspeth County.

Apaches made repeated attacks in the 1850s on travelers and mail coaches on the road between Fort Davis and San Elizario. This was part of the main road between San Antonio and El Paso and travelers expected some protection.

Captain Arthur Lee and 86 men of the 8th Infantry established this post September 28, 1858, on the Rio Grande just upstream from the mouth of what has since been called Quitman Canyon. The road from El Paso followed the Rio Grande to this canyon and then followed the canyon. The soldiers built most of the buildings after the Army hired some Mexicans to teach them how to make adobes.

The fort was named for John A. Quitman. He had just died in Mississippi. He was a hero to the Army because of his service in Mexico. He was a hero to Texans because he had brought a company of volunteers to Nacogdoches at his own expense during the Texas Revolution. Quitman had also been a member of Congress, governor of Mississippi and military governor of Mexico City.

The Butterfield Overland Mail Line established a station in Quitman Canyon near the fort when the line changed its route in 1859. The size of the garrison was reduced to thirty men and one officer by the summer of 1860 and the officer in charge at the

beginning of the Civil War was Lieutenant Zenas R. Bliss. Some Union officers on the frontier joined the Confederacy. Bliss did not. He served with the 10th Rhode Island Volunteers on the Union side and he rose to the rank of colonel. He was back in Texas in 1869. He became commander of the Department of Texas and served at San Antonio, Fort Duncan, Fort Clark, Fort Davis and Fort Bliss. He was a major general when he retired in 1897.

Union troops returned to Fort Quitman in 1868. The adobe buildings were in poor condition and they never were completely rebuilt. The garrison was concerned mostly with escorting travelers until 1877 when the post was abandoned. Colonel Benjamin Grierson and his 10th Cavalry used Fort Quitman as an outpost during their campaign against Chief Victorio and his Apaches in 1879 and 1880. It was manned as a subpost of Fort Davis in 1881 and 1882.

A remnant of Victorio's band attacked a stagecoach near Fort Quitman after Victorio was killed in Mexico. The attack occured in January of 1881. The Indians killed the stage driver and a passenger. Texas Rangers tracked the Apaches down and had it out with them in Victoria Canyon, 25 miles north of what is now Van Horn in what is now Culberson County. It was the last Indian fight of any consequence in this part of Texas and the Rangers won.

The original Fort Quitman was built of adobe. A truck stop operator built an adobe replica of the fort on I-10 east of McNary, as a tourist attraction. It was not a success and it was demolished in 1985.

FORT STOCKTON

Rooney and 5th streets, city of Fort Stockton, Pecos County.

This is the only U. S. Army fort in Texas named for a naval officer. Robert Field Stockton was a graduate of the U.S. Naval Academy, commander of the U.S. Pacific Fleet during the Mexican War and later a member of the U.S. Senate. Stockton brought to Texas in 1845 the first U.S. offer of annexation. It is not clear what prompted the Army to name a frontier fort for him. It is perfectly plain why the Army put the fort here, but not as plain why it was so late in doing so.

The location is on Comanche Creek, near Comanche Springs. The road between San Antonio and El Paso crossed the Great Comanche War Trail here. It was an important water hole and a dangerous place to stop.

Troops were stationed here a little earlier but the post was established March 23, 1859 by Lieutenant Walter Jones and a company of the 1st Infantry. It was called Camp Stockton when it was established. The name was changed to Fort Stockton the same year.

The original buildings were adobe, on stone foundations, with thatch and canvas roofs. There were three barracks buildings and five houses for the officers. This was one base where gardening was successful.

The garrison at Fort Stockton provided escorts for travelers and discouraged Indian attacks just by being here. It was not equipped for chasing Indians. The Butterfield Overland Mail Line had a stop here after 1859. The mail coaches came

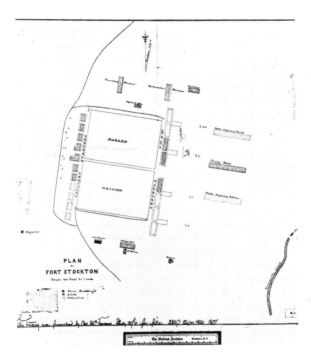

This sketch of Fort Stockton in the National Archives is dated 1871. It indicates the fort was about half finished at that time. The post was abandoned 15 years later.

Opposite: The barracks and stables are all gone. But Fort Stockton's stone guardhouse is still standing.

through twice a week. Mail from Fort Stockton took fifteen days to reach Washington, going by coach to Tipton, Missouri, and by train from there.

The 2nd Texas Mounted Rifles occupied the post for a little while during the Civil War. But there was no coach traffic and little else to defend this far west. The frontier defense line was pulled back early in the war. The buildings were in ruins when the federal troops returned in 1867. The Confederates may have set fire to the fort when they withdrew, but the damage could have been done by vandals. Several of the frontier forts became hangouts for draft dodgers and Union sympathizers during the war.

The buildings were rebuilt. The new Fort Stockton had five houses for officers, four barracks, a hospital and a guardhouse built of stone and adobe. Black troops of the 9th Cavalry and the 24th Infantry were stationed here after the war. The fort had outposts at Escondidos, Rainbow Cliffs and Frazier's Ranch.

The Indians were bolder after the war. There were two attacks on stage coaches in this area the same year the soldiers returned. Attacks continued into the 1870s. The Indians sometimes would duck across the border after making a raid. The soldiers sometimes followed them, despite the complaints of Mexican authorities.

The present town of Fort Stockton grew out of the trading post at the fort. The troops left in 1886. The buildings became the property of the land owners. The government had only leased the site.

Three of the adobe officers' houses are still standing and in good condition. The house in the right foreground is privately owned. The other two are owned and maintained by the city of Fort Stockton.

Captain Henry Carroll commanded the troops of the 9th Cavalry stationed at Fort Stockton after the Civil War.

THE EFFECT OF THE STAGE LINES AND THE CIVIL WAR

The frontier was advancing gradually in the 1850s. The mail companies were the skirmish lines of civilization. Senator Tom Rusk of Texas was on the Post Office Committee and he was one of the champions of the western mail companies until he killed himself in 1857.

Henry Skillman was still the chief mail contractor in west Texas in 1854 when the Post Office Department suddenly called for new bids and awarded a man named David Wasson the contract for hauling the mail between Sante Fe and San Antonio. Wasson had no equipment. He had to borrow money from George Giddings of San Antonio to get his service started. Wasson couldn't pay the money back. Giddings took over the line and worked out a deal with Skillman. They were operating the mail and passenger line together by the fall of 1854 and losing money. Wasson had bid too low. Giddings reported in 1855 that the line had lost 350 horses and mules in the first year, had two men killed and suffered property damage of more than $50,000. The Post Office Department raised the compensation but Giddings and Skillman were still losing money and on top of that, they had to pay a fine every time they were late with the mail, regardless of the reason.

The mail between California and the East was still moving by ship and the service was very slow. People in California petitioned for overland service. Congress had already approved the idea when President James Buchanan took office in 1857. Buchanan named A.V. Brown of Tennessee postmaster general and Brown took over the job of awarding the first contract for overland mail to California.

Congress apparently meant for the successful bidder to choose the route. But the new postmaster general chose the contractor and then told him what the route would be. The contract went to a company headed by John Butterfield and Brown specified that the route would be through El Paso. Critics said Butterfield got the contract because he was a friend of Buchanan and they said Brown chose the southern route because he was a southerner laying the groundwork for a southern transcontinental railroad. The critics may have been right on both counts. But the administration could have made worse choices. Butterfield was 56 when he got the contract. He had operated stage lines in the East. He helped create the American Express Company when he merged his line with the lines operated by Wells and Company and the Livingston and Fargo line in 1849. He knew what he was doing and he needed a new place to do it because the railroads had taken over the passenger and freight business in the East by 1857.

Butterfield took a very personal interest in organizing the new line. He and his associates sold stock and raised two million dollars. They hired 800 people to build and improve roads, dig wells and set up stations and corrals along the route. Butterfield had planned to use a more northerly route, through Albuquerque, when he put in his bid. But he accepted the postmaster general's decision and laid out a route from the end of the rail line at Tipton, Missouri, to San Francisco. This route entered Texas at Colbert's Ferry on the Red River and ran through Jacksboro, Fort

OVERLAND TO THE PACIFIC.

The San Antonio and San Diego Mail-Line.

This Line, which has been in successful operation since July, 1857, is ticketing PASSENGERS through to San Diego and San Francisco, and also to all intermediate stations. Passengers and Express matter forwarded in NEW COACHES, drawn by six mules, over the entire length of our Line, excepting the Colorado Desert of one hundred miles, which we cross on mule-back. Passengers GUARANTEED in their tickets to ride in Coaches, excepting the one hundred miles above stated.

Passengers ticketed through, from NEW-ORLEANS, to the following points, via SAN ANTONIO:

To Fort Clark,	Fare, $52.	To Fort Bliss,	Fare, $100.
" Hudson,	" 60.	" La Mesilla,	" 105.
" Fort Lancaster,	" 70.	" Fort Fillmore,	" 105.
" Davis,	" 90.	" Tucson,	" 135.
" Quitman,	" 100.	" Fort Yuma,	" 162.
" Birchville,	" 100.	" San Diego,	" 190.
" San Elizario,	" 100.	" Los Angelos,	" 190.
" El Paso,	" 100.	" San Francisco,	" 200.

The Coaches of our Line leave semi-monthly from each end, on the 9th and 24th of each month, at 6 o'clock A.M.

An armed escort travels through the Indian country with each mail train, for the protection of the mails and passengers.

Passengers are provided with provisions during the trip, except where the Coach stops at Public Houses along the Line, at which each Passenger will pay for his own meal.

Each Passenger is allowed thirty pounds of personal baggage, exclusive of blankets and arms.

Passengers coming to San Antonio can take the line of mail-steamers from New-Orleans five times a week to Indianola. From the latter place there is a daily line of four-horse mail-coaches direct to this place.

On the Pacific side, the California Steam Navigation Company are running a first-class steamer, semi-monthly, to and from San Francisco and San Diego.

Extra Baggage, *when carried*, 40 cents per pound to El Paso, and $1 per pound to San Diego.

Passengers can obtain all necessary outfits in San Antonio.

For further information, and for the purchase of tickets, apply at the office of C. G. WAYNE, 61 Camp Street, New-Orleans, or at the Company's Office, in San Antonio.

G. H. GIDDINGS,
R. E. DOYLE, } Proprietors.

George Giddings' advertisements promised passengers they would have armed escorts through Indian country.

Belknap, Fort Phantom Hill, Fort Chadbourne, Camp Johnston, around the southern edge of the High Plain, to Castle Gap, to Horsehead Crossing on the Pecos.

The original Butterfield Road did not cross the Pecos at Horsehead. It ran up the east bank of the river to Pope's Camp, crossed the river there and ran west through what is now the Guadalupe Mountains National Park. The road crossed over the New Mexico line near Crow Spring and back into Texas again near Ojos de los Alamos, to what is now Hueco Tanks State Park and on to El Paso and California. Postmaster General Brown called it the longest and most important land route ever established in any country. It attracted international attention. The British press hailed it as a big time-saver for people sending mail between England and British Columbia.

The Butterfield Company had 250 coaches built by J.S. Abbott and Sons of Concord, New Hampshire; James Gould of Albany, New York and Eaton, Gilbert and Company of Troy, New York. The Butterfield Line did not use Concord coaches on the run across Texas. The Texas roads were not good enough. The Butterfield passengers traveled across Texas in plainer coaches with smaller wheels and a lower center of gravity. These vehicles were known as celerity wagons. They had canvas tops. The seats could be folded down to make a large bed. The company built 139 stations on the original route and eventually there were 200 stations. But there were no overnight stops. The stations were to provide meals and fresh mules. The Butterfield coaches traveled day and night. Passengers had to get what sleep they could on the road, for three weeks if they were going all the way from Missouri to

Markers still stand all across the West as reminders of the way things were before the railroads. This marker is in Shackelford County.

California. They could stop over at one of the stations but they couldn't be sure there would be room for them on the next coach.

The fare originally was $200 from Missouri to California and $100 from California to Missouri. It was the law of supply and demand. More people wanted to go west than wanted to go east. Later the fare was changed to $150 each way. The main business of the Butterfield Line was carrying the mail and everything else was subordinate to that. The drivers were all issued bugles they were supposed to use to signal their approach so the stock handlers at the stations could have the fresh teams in harness and ready to be hitched to the coach when it arrived. John Butterfield regularly reminded his drivers and supervisors: "Nothing on God's earth must stop the United States Mail."

The Butterfield stations were about 20 miles apart. Some of them were simply houses. Some of them were adjacent to forts and some of them were miniature forts themselves, depending upon the degree of exposure to Indian attacks. The coaches were supposed to cover about 120 miles every 24 hours. They were pulled by two, four or six mules, depending upon the load and the terrain. The company favored mules over horses because the mules were a little less likely to be stolen by the Comanches. The Comanches would eat mules but no Comanche would be seen riding one.

The Butterfield Overland Mail Line started operating in September of 1858. The first coach left California September 15 with five passengers. The first coach left Tipton, Missouri, September 16. John Butterfield personally took the mail bags from the train at Tipton and delivered them to the stage coach. John Butterfield, Jr. drove the coach the first 300 miles and John Sr. rode the coach that far. The only passenger to go all the way to California on the first westbound Butterfield coach was a newspaper reporter named Walter Ormsby, writing for the *New York Herald*.

One of the passengers on the first coach from California was a Post Office Department special agent named Bailey. His report to the postmaster general was full of praise for the contractor's energy and perseverance. He observed that the company was traveling an extra hundred miles by skirting around the southern edge of the High Plain between Fort Belknap and the Pecos River but he thought this was understandable, considering the shortage of water and the surplus of Comanches on the High Plain. This is the same plain also often called Llano Estacado.

John Butterfield was waiting in Tipton when the first coach from California arrived there October 9. President Buchanan sent a telegram of congratulations calling the service a great triumph for civilization and the Union.

The Overland Mail Road was named for Butterfield. His is the name most often associated with stage lines. But John Butterfield headed the Overland Mail Company for less than two years. The bookkeepers thought he was to extravagant. They pushed him out and put one of their kind in his place, as bookkeepers will do. The Butterfield Overland Mail Line was just another mail and stage line after that, and it still wasn't making any money.

George Giddings was carrying mail and passengers by 1857 between San Antonio and San Diego and between El Paso and Santa Fe. The new postmaster general rewrote Giddings' contract and gave John Birch authority to carry the mail between San Antonio and San Diego. Birch hired a qualified manager and started service.

But Birch died in a shipwreck before the new line got going well. Giddings got Birch's widow to sign the contract over to him. The line hadn't made any money. She evidently was glad to get rid of it.

There was no direct competition between the Giddings Line and the Butterfield Overland. The Butterfield coaches did not serve San Antonio, San Diego or Santa Fe. The Giddings' coaches did not go to San Francisco.

The Post Office Department scaled Giddings' contract down in 1859 so that he was carrying mail only between San Antonio and El Paso and between Fort Yuma and San Diego.

Postmaster General Brown died in 1859. He was succeeded by an economizer named Joseph Holt. He was soon looking for ways to save money on the mail contracts. Holt ordered the Butterfield Overland to change its route to the south, to stop at Comanche Springs (Fort Stockton) and follow from there to El Paso the road Giddings had been using, through Fort Davis. The Butterfield Overland Company was not unhappy about this. There were more customers and there was better protection on the southern route. Giddings was unhappy. He was left with just a contract between San Antonio and Comanche Springs, where his coaches turned the mail over to the Butterfield Overland. He didn't need any authority from the Post Office to carry passengers on to the coast, though, and he continued to do that.

Roscoe and Margaret Conkling made an exhaustive study of the Butterfield Overland Mail Line in the 1930s. They drove a 1930 Buick over the entire route and

The Pecos River carried much more water in the early days before dams were built. Crossing it was dangerous. Horsehead Crossing supposedly got its name from the number of horse skulls littering the banks.

located all the old Butterfield stations. They said in their book, *The Butterfield Overland Mail*, that there was only one recorded instance of an Indian attack on a Butterfield coach. That was in Arizona in 1861. But there were Indian attacks on the Skillman and Gidding coaches. Henry Skillman killed an Apache with his Sharps rifle in 1852 at a spot outside of Fort Davis that is still called Skillman's Grove. Skillman worked for all the subsequent stage operators. *New York Herald* writer Walter Ormsby marveled in print over Skillman's stamina. Ormsby said in his report on the first Butterfield run to California that Skillman took over the reins at Horsehead Crossing on the Pecos and drove all the way to Franklin (El Paso). That was more than 200 miles, including some mountain roads. Skillman was 44 at the time, in 1858. He was dead six years later. Union soldiers ambushed him and killed him near Presidio in 1864. Skillman was running a courier service on the border. The Yankees thought he was spying for the Confederates. That would not have been out of character.

The biggest expense items the stage line operators had were livestock and feed. Some of the stage stations were miles from sources of hay and grain. The Apaches and Comanches nearly always set fire to the hay when they raided the corrals at the stage stations. They stole the horses and scattered the mules more often than they attacked the station personnel. But they attacked the personnel, too. Apache attacks on the station at Eagle Springs in the mountains in what is now southeastern Hudspeth County killed three station hands in 1856 and two in 1858.

An Apache band led by Chief Jose Maria made the mistake of attacking a convoy of freight wagons on the road near Fort Quitman in February of 1859. The freighters and their military escort fought off the attack and killed the chief. They left Jose Maria's body hanging from a tree beside the road, twisting in the wind as a warning to other Indians.

Slaveholders always were a minority in Texas. But nearly everybody in Texas believed in states' rights. Sentiment for secession was rising before the election of

Ben McCulloch took part in every fight Texas had from the time he got here in 1836 until he was killed in 1862. He was at San Jacinto. He fought with the Rangers against the Indians. He was with Zachary Taylor in Mexico. He was a brigadier general in the Confederate Army when he was killed in action. Ben McCulloch engineered the capture of all the federal forts in Texas at the start of the Civil War.

1860. The election of Abraham Lincoln was the last straw. Governor Sam Houston did all he could to dissuade them, but secessionists organized conventions in the counties and elected delegates to meet in a Secession Convention in Austin, January 28, 1861. The Secessionists so dominated the local meeetings that very few opponents of secession made it to Austin. The convention voted January 29 to recommend secession. A referendum was scheduled for February 23.

There were 2328 U.S. soldiers stationed at 19 federal forts within the state. The secession strategists didn't wait for the election. The convention established a Committee of Public Safety to take over all federal property in Texas.

Ben McCulloch was a key member of the Committee of Public Safety. He appeared in San Antonio with 400 volunteers on February 8 and called on the commander of the Department of Texas to surrender his troops and forts. The commander was General David Twiggs, former commander of the 2nd Dragoons, hero of the Mexican War. He would say later that he had asked Washington the previous December what he should do if this happend. He said General Winfield Scott never answered him. Twiggs engaged the secessionists in conversation until February 15. McCulloch moved his volunteers into Alamo Plaza that night and they captured and disarmed 160 U.S. soldiers. The morning of the 16th, Twiggs agreed to leave Texas if his troops could take their arms and personal property with them. McCullough kept up the pressure until Twiggs agreed on February 18 to surrender all the federal forts and property, ordnance, wagons, animals and supplies. Twiggs was promised his troops would be allowed to leave and most of them did move out through the port of Indianola. But units of the 8th Infantry stationed at the far western posts — Bliss, Stockton, Davis, Quitman and Lancaster — didn't reach San Antonio until the other Union troops had departed. They were imprisoned and later exchanged for Confederates captured by Union forces.

Most of the enlisted men stayed with the Union. Many of the officers resigned to join the Confederate forces. General Twiggs didn't have to resign. He was summarily dismissed from the U.S. Army and branded a scoundrel. Twiggs was 71. He would

General David Emmanuel Twiggs was in command of all federal forces in Texas in 1861, with headquarters in San Antonio. Texas volunteers led by Ben McCulloch forced him to surrender all the forts before Texas actually seceded from the Union. Twiggs was immediately dismissed from the Union Army. He immediately joined the Confederate army.

have been retired a hero before 1861 if the Army had had a retirement program. He joined the Confederate Army as a major general but he resigned a year later and died in July 1862 in his native Georgia.

Colonel Robert E. Lee passed through San Antonio on his way from Fort Mason to Washington immediately after Twiggs' surrender. The secessionists tried to pursuade Lee to join them. He said he felt obliged to carry out his orders to report to Washington. He was allowed to leave — minus his baggage, according to one report. Lee didn't resign from the U.S. Army until his native Virginia seceded.

Texas voters ratified the decision to secede February 23. The secession was effective March 2, on the 25th anniversary of the Texas Declaration of Independence. Sam Houston was removed from the governor's office. Lieutenant Governor Edward Clark became governor and Texans embarked upon the course Sam Houston had warned them against.

William B. Dinsmore was president of the Butterfield Overland Mail Line. He never had as much style as John Butterfield but he recognized that it was time to get out of Texas. The company asked the Post Office Department on March 2, 1861, to annul its contract and give it a new route. The last eastbound coach passed through Denton on March 14. Russell, Majors and Waddell Company was carrying the mail between St. Louis and California by way of Colorado and Utah. The Post Office Department worked out a plan to have Russell, Majors and Waddell handle the run from St. Louis to Salt Lake City. The Butterfield Overland Mail Line became responsible for hauling the mail between Salt Lake City and San Francisco. The line never returned to Texas. Much of the company's equipment was left in Texas. Some of it was bought by George Giddings. The first shot hadn't been fired at Fort Sumter, yet. Many people doubted there would be a war. George Giddings evidently was one of those people.

President Lincoln appointed John Blair to be postmaster general. Blair had been Giddings' lobbyist in Washington. Giddings easily got a contract to haul the U.S. mail between San Antonio and Los Angeles. The first coach to make the run in May of 1861 was attacked by Apaches near Fort Davis. Giddings was in the coach. Everybody survived that attack, but Giddings' brother James was killed by Apaches in New Mexico a little later. Two people were killed in an Indian raid on the stage station at Eagle Springs. This service was abandoned as soon as the war began. Giddings had lost 30 men, six coaches and 100 horses by then. Major James Longstreet rode one of Giddings' coaches, before the service ended, on his way from his U.S. Army post at Albuquerque to New Orleans where he offered his services to the Confederacy.

George Giddings got the Confederate Post Office Department to give his stage coach company a contract to haul mail between San Antonio and El Paso. The Union army occupied El Paso and that was the end of that. But Giddings was a survivor. He got several other Confederate mail contracts and stayed busy until the Confederacy collapsed. He started hauling freight for the Union army after the war. This apparently was more profitable than hauling passengers and mail. W.R. Austerman says in his history of the San Antonio Mail Line that Giddings never bid on another mail contract.

People continued to travel to California throughout the Civil War. The U.S. Army continued to fight Indians and the frontier continued to move west, but not in Texas. An entrepreneur named Ben Holladay took over the operations of Russell, Majors and Waddell and the Overland Mail Line in 1862. He consolidated them into the Overland Stage Line. The Indians Holladay had to deal with were Sioux, Arapaho and Cheyenne. They were almost as troublesome as Comanches and Apaches. Holladay had to suspend service for a while in 1864 because of Indian attacks in Colorado.

President Lincoln wanted the overland mail service continued because the only alternative was steamer mail and he thought that was more susceptible to Confederate interference. But the U.S. Army still had no effective plan for controlling the Indians.

The commanders on the central plains in 1863 and 1864 were still sending out large columns of troops to scout for Indians. The Indians simply avoided them, most of the time. Colonel Kit Carson and his 1st New Mexico Volunteer Cavalry did catch a band of Comanches and Kiowas at an old buffalo hunters' camp called Abode Walls, in the Texas Panhandle, in the fall of 1864.

Carson made an attack. He had underestimated the number of Indians by almost 3000. He lost two men and he thought he killed 60 Indians. But he abandoned the attack and withdrew. It was a fight he was not going to win. It would be another 10 years before the army could claim to have the Comanches under control. But the

This picture from the files of the Institute of Texan Cultures is said to show the Texas volunteer force that persuaded General Twiggs he had no choice except to surrender.

Navajos were subdued during the Civil War. The U.S. Army captured thousands of Confederate soldiers during the war. They were not all held in prison camps. Some of them were pressed into service with the Union forces. They were not trusted to serve in areas where they would be opposing Confederate forces. They were sent to the western frontier to fight Indians. They were known as Galvanized Yankees.

The Confederate government made a stab at raising troops to defend the Texas frontier but never followed through. State troops were stationed initially at Fort Davis, Fort Stockton, Fort Lancaster, Camp Hudson, Fort Mason, Fort Inge, Fort Duncan, Camp Verde and Camp Wood. The legislature authorized the frontier counties to raise their own defense forces. These were disbanded in 1862 when a state militia was organized. The Texas Frontier Regiment was the chief component of the militia. The frontier defense line was pulled back. State authorities decided to try to defend a line running from Fort Belknap to Camp Verde to Fort Inge to Fort Duncan. Lawyer James Norris was named by Governor Francis Lubbock to command the Frontier Regiment. Historian W.C. Holden says Norris' method of defending the frontier was to have his troops make continuous patrols between the posts. The troops didn't like Norris and they didn't like his strategy and his strategy didn't work. The Indians figured it out and scheduled their raids when the patrols were somewhere else.

Colonel J.E. McCord was elected to command the Frontier Regiment when Norris resigned in January of 1863. McCord's strategy was to send patrols out into the Indian country at irregular intervals. This didn't work very well, either. The frontier defense scheme was revamped in December of 1863 and again in May of 1864. The state started drafting men for the frontier defense forces in 1863. Some of the men eligible for the draft were Union sympathizers and some just didn't want to be drafted. Many of these people drifted to the frontier. Governor Pendleton Murrah

ordered the frontier closed to immigration because of this. W.C. Holden says the frontier defense system never really broke down completely during the war, the way it did during the first two years of the Union occupation after the war.

The biggest fiasco the state defense forces were involved in occurred in the final year of the war a few miles south of the present city of San Angelo. Texas scouts discovered a big band of Indians traveling through and assumed they were up to no good. About 350 frontier troopers led by Captain Henry Fossett took out after the Indians and attacked them. The Indians were Kickapoos migrating from the Oklahoma Indian Territory to Mexico. They were not looking for trouble. But there were 1400 of them and they had no trouble fighting off the Texans. Thirty-six Texans were killed and 60 were wounded in what was called the Battle of Dove Creek.

The defense forces along the Mexican border gave a better account of themselves. The character of the border commander had much to do with this. John Salmon Ford was in command on the border from start to finish. He was a veteran of the Texas Army and the Texas Rangers. He was popular; fearless but not flamboyant. His nickname had nothing to do with his personality. Everybody called him Rip Ford. It was because he had to send out a lot of death notices when his Texas Ranger force was with the U.S. Army during the Mexican War. He always included the phrase Rest In Peace in these messages. This was often abbreviated R.I.P.

Rip Ford was a militant secessionist. He was a key member of the Committee of Public Safety that took over the federal forts and federal property during the prelude to secession. He accepted the surrender of Fort Brown. He took part in the last battle of the Civil War. This was the Battle of Palmito Ranch (Palmito Hill). It occurred when Confederate cavalry attacked 300 Union troops as they were marching from the mouth of the Rio Grande toward Brownsville. Colonel Ford arrived on the scene with reinforcements and a half-dozen cannon. The Union troops wisely abandoned the field and hastened back to their camp at the mouth of the river. They didn't venture out again until they were assured that Colonel Ford and the Confederates had been informed how things stood. The Union troops knew when they set out to occupy Fort Brown that Lee had surrendered and the war was over. Ford and the Confederates didn't know it until after they had fought and won the Battle of Palmito Hill, May 13, 1865.

There was less effort put into defending the Texas frontier in the immediate aftermath of the Civil War than at any time between 1849 and 1861. U.S. troops returned to Texas but they did not return to the frontier. They were more concerned with standing watch over the populated sections of the state, defending the rights of liberated slaves and supervising elections. The frontier moved backward 100 miles

A buffalo hunters' camp called Adobe Walls was the scene of two major battles between whites and Indians. Kit Carson and his New Mexico Cavalry failed to dislodge a band of Comanches from the camp in the fall of 1864. The Indians fought him to a standstill.

in some places in 1866 and 1867. Texans were not allowed to organize any frontier defense force because the U.S. Army didn't like the idea of organized groups of Texans with firearms anywhere in the occupied territory. Settlers on the frontier moved closer together and some left. Many were killed or kidnapped by Indians. They didn't get much sympathy from the U.S. Army. General Sherman said every little settlement wanted at least a regiment. He wasn't disposed to send any help at all and he might never have sent any except for the pressure from other citizens.

The end of the Civil War made the southern route to California usable again. Wagon trains were rolling across the plains of Texas. Stage lines were starting up again. Bethel Coopwood started a line between San Antonio and El Paso in April of 1866. The first coach to make the run from San Antonio had 40 armed guards. The party was attacked by Apaches at Escondido Springs just west of the Pecos. The escorts drove the Indians off but it took two days.

Coopwood sold his line to Sawyer, Risher and Hall before the end of 1866 and Ben Ficklin took over management of the service in 1867. Ficklin had had a lot of experience. He had been a superintendent on the Central Overland and Pike's Peak Express during the Civil War and he had worked for the Pony Express. Ficklin expanded his service over the next few years until he was operating over substantially the same route the Butterfield Overland had used. He had branch lines serving many other areas. One of his lines ran between San Antonio and Fort Stockton by way of Leon Springs, Boerne, Fredericksburg, Mason and Fort Concho. The Ficklin Line had a station in the old Nimitz Hotel in Fredericksburg. Ficklin was

carrying the mail three times a week over the old Butterfield route by 1868. He was the biggest factor in west Texas transportation and he ran his business personally.

Austerman says Ficklin showed up at Fort Davis once driving himself in a light wagon in an area where prudent people didn't travel without an armed escort.

Ficklin had his San Antonio station on Alamo Plaza. He built a big stable right across from the Alamo. He continued to run the stage and mail line until he died in 1870 at the age of 43.

The U.S. Army had reorganized its mounted forces at the outset of the Civil War. The 1st Dragoons became the 1st Cavalry. The old 1st Cavalry became the 4th Cavalry. The 2nd Dragoons became the 2nd Cavalry. The old 2nd Cavalry became the 5th Cavalry. The old Mounted Rifles became the 3rd Cavalry. More cavalry regiments were added during the war. The Army started enlisting black soldiers during the war and organized six black regiments after the war. Among them were the 9th and 10th Cavalry and the 24th and 25th Infantry. The officers were all white. The enlisted men were all black, many of them former slaves. All four of these regiments would see service on the Texas frontier.

The first U.S. troops detailed to the frontier after the Civil War were the men of the 4th and 6th Cavalry regiments. Governor J.W. Throckmorton insisted upon more protection.

The 4th Cavalry was ordered to Fort Mason in 1866, to guard the frontier between the Colorado River and Fort Clark. The 6th Cavalry was sent to Jacksboro with orders to protect the area between the Red River and Camp Cooper. This was a temporary arrangement until decisions could be made about which of the frontier forts should be reoccupied.

The 9th Cavalry was ordered to reoccupy the old forts on the upper Rio Grande, with headquarters at Fort Stockton. The white officers of the 9th Cavalry were experienced. The enlisted men were new to the Army and new to Texas. The 4th Cavalry was the old 2nd Cavalry. It had been the outstanding outfit on the frontier before the Civil War. But it, too, was made up mostly of green recruits in 1867. These were the men out front as the Army resumed the war with the Texas Indians.

Right: John Butterfield's mail coaches made the run betweeen Missouri and California within the required 25 days, more often than not. He had to pay a penalty if they were late.

Opposite: Seven hundred mounted Plains Indians bent on stopping the slaughter of the buffalo attacked the camp at Adobe Walls June 27, 1874. There were just 28 hunters in the camp but they were superbly armed, as buffalo hunters always were. They broke up the attack and drove the Indians off. This was the beginning of the end of the reign of the Plains Indians.

Fort Richardson
Fort Griffin
Fort Concho
Fort Elliott
Fort Sam Houston
Camp Pena Colorado
Fort Hancock

THE LAST FRONTIER FORTS AND THE END OF THE INDIAN WAR

The U.S. Army built three new forts soon after the troops returned to the Texas frontier following the Civil War. The concept in Washington at the time was to maintain a barrier between the white settlements and the Indian hunting grounds. But the Indians continued to raid white settlements and white settlers continued to covet the Indian hunting grounds. These new forts became bases for what finally became a campaign to eliminate the Indians from Texas. The forts were Richardson, Griffin and Concho.

Texans were still complaining about the Indian problem in 1871, five years after the U.S. troops had returned to the frontier.

General William T. Sherman was in command of all Army forces west of the Mississippi. He decided to find out whether the Indian problem really was as bad as the Texans claimed it was. Sherman came to Texas and started an inspection of the frontier forts, traveling from south to north. He saw some abandoned and burned out homesteads. He heard stories about how many people had been killed and wounded in Indian raids and about how many people had given up and moved away. There will always be some question about what the general's overall impression might have been if it hadn't been for what happened at Fort Richardson.

Sherman was at Richardson May 19, 1871, when a teamster named Thomas Brazeal limped in to report an Indian attack on a wagon train the day before. The wagon train was one hauling supplies to Fort Richardson for government contractor Henry Warren. It was making its way along the Salt Creek flats between Fort Griffin and Fort Richardson when it was attacked by a band of Kiowas and Comanches.

The Indians killed the wagonmaster and six teamsters. Brazeal was one of five survivors. General Sherman had ridden the same route the wagon train was traveling only the day before.

The Indians responsible for the attack on the Warren wagon train were residents of the reservations in Indian Territory. One of the complaints Texans had been

General William T. Sherman had a close call on a visit to the Texas frontier in 1871 and it helped change the U.S. Indian policy.

making was that the reservation Indians left the reservations to make raids into Texas any time it suited them. The United States government at the time was counting on Quaker Indian Agents to manage the reservations and the Indians. The Quakers had a hard time believing their Indians could do the awful things Texans claimed they did. But General Sherman believed it after May 18. Colonel Ranald Mackenzie was in command of Fort Richardson. Sherman and nearly everybody else considered Mackenzie one of the ablest officers in the Army. He was the right man to do the job Sherman wanted done.

The General told the Colonel to go after the Indians responsible for the wagon train raid. Sherman continued on his inspection trip. Mackenzie started his pursuit of the Indians. The Indians got back to the reservation before Mackenzie caught up with

Ranald Slidell Mackenzie played the key role in the final showdown with the Comanche and Kiowa Indians and their allies. He beat the Comanches by separating them from their horses.

them. Sherman was at Fort Sill when three chiefs came in there bragging about their raid. The Army did not normally have any jurisdiction over Indians on a reservation. No federal Indian agent had ever allowed an Indian to be arrested on a reservation. But agent Laurie Tatum decided it was justified in this case. He allowed Sherman's soldiers to arrest Chief Satanta, Chief Satank and Chief Big Tree. Satank was killed trying to escape. Satanta and Big Tree were the first Indians tried for murder in a white man's court. The courts were not granting changes of venue because of local prejudice against the defendants then. The trial was held where the feelings against the defendants were the strongest. Both chiefs were convicted in Jacksboro next door to Fort Richardson and sentenced to death.

President Grant intervened at the urging of the Bureau of Indian Affairs. He asked carpetbag Governor Edmund Davis to commute the sentences and Davis did. Satanta and Big Tree were in prison at Huntsville when the president made another

Three Kiowa chiefs touched off the Army's campaign against their tribe and the Comanches when they led a murderous raid into Texas while General Sherman was touring the frontier. Sherman had the chiefs arrested. Satank *(Opposite)* was killed trying to escape. Satanta *(Top)* and Big Tree *(Bottom)* were the first Indians to be tried for murder in a Texas court.

request. He wanted the two chiefs paroled. Davis paroled them in 1873 over the strenuous protests of General Sherman. Big Tree got religion and caused no more trouble. Satanta was accused of leading an attack on buffalo hunters and he was sent back to Huntsville where he killed himself October 11, 1878, by jumping out a second-story window.

General Sherman didn't stop with punishing the chiefs responsible for the raid on the Warren wagon train. He encouraged Ranald Mackenzie to wage a general war on the Plains Indians in Texas. Colonel Mackenzie was back in the Panhandle in the fall of 1871 and again in 1872. He surprised a band of Comanches in camp on the North Fork of the Red River in the fall of 1872. He killed a few of the Indians and scattered the others and captured 500 horses. The Comanches stole the horses back the same night and taught Mackenzie an important lesson.

Top: The headquarters of the Kiowa — Comanche Agency, near Fort Sill in Indian Territory, where Satank, Santanta and Big Tree were arrested. They were surprised. Indians previously had been immune to arrest on their reservations. They expected to get away with murder.

Opposite: Ranald Mackenzie's cavalry surprised Quanah Parker's Comanches in their camp on the floor of Palo Duro Canyon near the present Palo Duro Canyon State Park. The Comanches never disturbed the peace in the Panhandle again.

Officials in Washington, for years, took a calm view of the reports of Indian livestock thefts in Texas. People there thought Texans were exaggerating. Historian J. Evetts Haley says they just couldn't imagine what a few thousand Indians could do with hundreds of thousands of cows and horses. The Indians were delivering the stolen livestock to traders from New Mexico. These traders were known as Comancheros. They brought guns and ammunition, whiskey and trinkets to the Panhandle, swapped them for cattle and horses and took the animals back to New Mexico for sale.

The main source of food for the Plains Indians always was the buffalo. The slaughter of the buffalo by white hide-hunters convinced the Indians by 1874 that

they were going to become wholly dependent upon government handouts if they didn't do something. Leaders of the Comanches, Kiowas, Arapahoes and the Cheyennes agreed to wage a joint war on the white buffalo hunters. The Indians had been promised in the Treaty of Medicine Lodge in 1867 that they would have exclusive rights to hunt the buffalo on the High Plain. But the U.S. government made that treaty and the High Plain was under Texas' jurisdiction. The Army was unofficially encouraging the slaughter of the buffalo by the 1870s. The Texas legislature considered a bill to prohibit the wholesale slaughter. The bill was dropped after General Philip Sheridan personally explained to the lawmakers that killing off the buffalo was the best way to get rid of the Plains Indians. The Indians would have

Texas governor Edmund J. Davis pardoned and then parolled Satanta and Big Tree at the insistence of Federal authorities. Davis had little choice. It was the carpetbag period and he was Washington's man.

to stop the slaughter themselves, if it was to be stopped. And they tried. Chief Quanah Parker led his Comanches and their allies in an attack on a buffalo hunters' camp at Adobe Walls in the Panhandle in June of 1874. The Indians greatly outnumbered the hunters. But the hunters had better rifles and shelter. The Indian attack failed.

The Indian alliance broke up but the Indians continued to attack the white hunters wherever they found them. This brought on a major Army campaign in the fall of 1874. Five task forces took the field to surround and subdue the Indians in the Panhandle. Colonel Nelson Miles and Lieutenant Colonel J.W. Davidson led a column

Quanah Parker was the last war chief of the most warlike branch of the Comanche tribe. He was half Indian. His mother was a white girl the Comanches kidnapped when she was nine years old. She was Cynthia Ann Parker.

each from Indian Territory. Major W.R. Price brought a column from Fort Union, New Mexico; Lieutenant Colonel G.P. Buel led a column up from Fort Griffin and Colonel Ranald Mackenzie brought the 4th Cavalry up from Fort Clark. Mackenzie was in overall charge and he delivered the knockout punch.

Mackenzie grabbed one of the Comanchero traders and forced him to reveal where Quanah Parker's Comanches had their camp. It was in the floor of the Palo Duro Canyon. Mackenzie's troopers surprised the Comanches there and managed to scatter them before they could get to their horses. Mackenzie had the horses shot so the Indians couldn't get them back. The Quahadis suffered through winter on the High Plain without horses. They gave up and moved to a reservation in the Indian Territory in the spring. This campaign is often called the Red River War because most of the action was in the area drained by tributaries of the Red River. It ended the Comanches' control of the High Plain.

The Army named the fort at Jacksboro for one of the Union generals killed in the Civil War. Israel Richardson was killed at Antietam.

FORT RICHARDSON

U.S. 281, ½-mile south of Jacksboro, Jack County.

The settlement of what is now the town of Jacksboro started in 1855, on the bank of Lost Creek in Jack County. The settlement was originally called Lost Creek. The name was changed later to Mesquiteville and it was being called Jacksborough by the time the Civil War started. The name was shortened to Jacksboro in 1899.

The Indian frontier was well to the west of Jacksborough in 1861 and there was no need for a fort.

But the Indians started ranging farther to the east during the Civil War when the frontier forts were abandoned. They ranged even farther east after 1865 when the

Most of the buildings at Fort Richardson were built of wood in the jacal, or picket, style.

state effort to defend the frontier collapsed. One source says more than 120 Texans were killed or wounded or taken prisoner by Indians between 1865 and 1867.

The U.S. Army started putting the frontier defense system back together in late 1866. The 6th Cavalry moved to Jacksborough and started planning a fort. The first idea was to locate it north of town at Buffalo Spring. But the water supply there was not dependable so a site was chosen on Lost Creek opposite the settlement.

The troops did some of the building. There were four barracks buildings and eight houses for officers. These were all timber. The bakery and the magazine, the

The cavalrymen stationed at Fort Richardson and the other posts on the Texas frontier had a lot of latitude in construing the uniform regulations. The standard Army uniforms were decidedly not suited to the Texas climate.

Fort Richardson was built on Lost Creek
opposite the settlement of Jacksboro, to
protect settlers and travelers on the road to
California. The frontier had moved back
this far during the Civil War.

General Philip Sheridan advised the Texas
legislature against interfering with the
slaughter of the buffalo on the Texas
plains. Sheridan thought slaughtering the
buffalo would help get rid of the Indians.

The Army left Fort Richardson in 1878. The Texas National Guard was using the post in the 1920s.

commissary warehouse, the quartermaster warehouse and the hospital were built of sandstone from a quarry on the site. The plans for the hospital were drawn in Washington. Fort Richardson was named for General Israel Richardson. He was fatally wounded by Confederates at the Battle of Antietam during the Civil War. The major buildings here were completed by 1869. A telegraph link with Fort Sill was completed in 1875. Most supplies came from Galveston by railroad to Calvert and then by wagon. The fort was manned by units of the 11th Infantry after the 6th Cavalry was transferred to Missouri in 1871.

There was no longer any need for a fort here after the Comanches were defeated in 1874. The troops moved to Fort Griffin in 1878. The city of Jacksboro acquired Fort Richardson later and gave it to the Texas Department of Parks and Wildlife in 1968. It is now a state park.

The post hospital was one of the few stone buildings built at Fort Richardson. It has been restored. The fort has been a state park since 1968.

FORT GRIFFIN

*U.S. 283, 15 miles north of
Albany, Shackelford County.*

Lieutenant Colonel Samuel Sturgis and four companies of the 6th Cavalry moved from Fort Belknap and established this post in July of 1867. They first chose a site on the bank of the Clear Fork of the Brazos and they named it Camp Wilson for Lieutenant Henry Wilson of the 6th Cavalry. The post was soon moved half a mile to a site with a little more elevation. The name was changed to Fort Griffin after Colonel Charles Griffin, acting commander of the Department of Texas when he died

Charles Griffin was acting commander of the Department of Texas when this post was established and it was named for him.

in September of 1867. The first buildings here were log and timber. A few later buildings were built of stone.

Ben Ficklin's stage and mail line had a station here. The mail came from the East on Sundays and Thursdays and from the West on Mondays and Thursdays. Letters mailed here could reach Washington in 12 days. Indians raided the stage line corrals here three times in the spring of 1869 and stole or scattered all the stock.

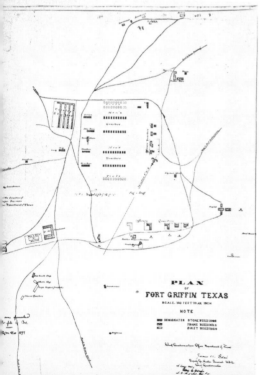

Top: A photograph made in the 1870s shows the site covered with buildings. It was a busy period on the far frontier.

Left: This sketch of the layout of Fort Griffin is dated 1871.

A band of Kiowas jumped a small wagon train hauling supplies to Fort Griffin in January of 1871. The Indians killed all four of the black teamsters and took their scalps. Troopers of the 6th Cavalry caught up with the Kiowas as they headed back to Indian Territory, but the Indians fought them off. One of the black teamsters killed that January 24th was Brit Johnson. The raid made a widow of the wife Johnson had rescued from the Kiowas and Comanches in 1864.

The troops stationed at Fort Griffin escorted the stage coaches and wagon trains and did what they could to protect the cattle drivers. Great herds of Texas longhorns were moving to northern pastures and northern markets by the late 1860s. The Western Cattle Trail to Dodge City came this way. White buffalo hunters were working the area by 1870, slaughtering the bison and shipping out wagon loads of hides.

Fort Griffin was one of the bases favored by the white buffalo hunters. They shipped tons of buffalo hides from here to Kansas for sale in the East. The settlement in this picture was just outside of Dodge City.

Hostile Indians still prowled the Plains in
the early 1870s. The soldiers at the frontier
posts had Indian scouts helping them keep
track of the hostile bands. Seminoles were
the scouts at some of the bases. Tonkawas
did the scouting for the garrison at Fort
Griffin where two of the scouts posed with
three young cavalrymen for this picture in
1870. Many of the soldiers of this period
were immigrants; some spoke less English
than the Indians.

There was traffic and there was some protection and there was money to be made. Saloon keepers, prostitutes and professional gamblers were always drawn to the places where such opportunities existed. There soon was a flourishing settlement outside Fort Griffin. It grew up on the river bank where Colonel Sturgis had first planned to build the fort. The settlement was called The Flat. Bat Masterson, Wyatt Earp, Pat Garret and Doc Holiday all were here at different times. Lotte Deno ran a poker game at The Flat for three years and then disappeared. Lotte was a legend and a mystery. She never told anyone her real name or where she came from or where she went from here. She evidently had the heart of gold women of her kind are often supposed to have. She left a note when she disappeared. It specified that the possessions she left behind were to be sold for the benefit of some needy person.

The hide business lasted only a few years. The cattle drives didn't last much longer. The Indians were not a serious threat after 1874. The settlement at the fort became the county seat when Shackelford County was organized in 1874. But the county

Only a few ruins still stand at Fort Griffin.
The site has been a state park since 1938.

government moved to Albany in 1875. The Army abandoned Fort Griffin in May of 1881. Albany had a railroad by then. The Flat never got a railroad. The Flat just died after the soldiers, cattle drivers and buffalo hunters departed.

The government never bought the land the fort occupied. The owners reclaimed it. The buildings fell down. Shackelford County acquired the property and donated it to the State Parks Board in 1936. It was designated a state park in 1938.

Barracks and parade ground at Fort Concho, about 1880. Civilians moved into the buildings here after the troops left in 1888, so most of the buildings survived.

FORT CONCHO

213 East Avenue D, San Angelo, Tom Green County.

This was another case where the Army picked an old Comanche watering place as the site for a fort. Lack of good water was the main shortcoming at Fort Chadbourne in what is now Coke County. An inspection board established by General Philip Sheridan recommended in November of 1867 that Fort Chadbourne be abandoned in favor of a new post on the Concho River. The units of the 4th Cavalry stationed at Chadbourne first set up an outpost at the headwaters of the Middle Concho. This was called Permanent Camp and it was abandoned when Captain George Hunt and 400 troopers established what was to become Fort Concho in December, 1867, at the junction of the North and South Conchos.

This post was first called Camp Hatch to honor Major John Hatch. He was a member of the inspection board that recommended the move. Hatch modestly

One barracks at Fort Concho has been
furnished approximately the way it would
have been furnished when the 10th
Cavalry was here in 1875.

suggested the name be changed. It was changed to Camp Kelly in honor of an officer killed by malaria at the Permanent Camp. The name was changed again in February of 1868 to Fort Concho. Nobody owned the land when the post was established but an alert settler filed a claim to it when the troops moved in and the Army started paying him rent.

The first buildings were timber but there was not much timber handy in 1867. Major John Hatch was in command briefly and he thought adobe was the best

The officers' quarters on the opposite side of the parade ground from the barracks have been restored and the parade ground is going to be restored to its 1880s condition. A public school, built in the middle of the parade ground years ago, is being demolished.

material for this site. He had the troops make thousands of adobe bricks but a rain came before they got anything built with them. Most of the adobes dissolved. The major was known as 'Dobe Hatch ever after. Most of the buildings eventually were built with local sandstone and much of the work was done by German craftsmen brought in from Fredericksburg.

Colonel Benjamin Grierson moved the headquarters of the 10th Cavalry here in 1875. Units of the 4th and 9th Cavalry had been stationed here earlier. Colonel Ranald Mackenzie moved the headquarters of the 4th Cavalry to Fort Richardson in 1871 to get closer to the Comanches. Mackenzie and his cavalrymen had tangled with a band of several hundred Indians on a patrol out of Fort Concho in 1869. They reported they killed 75 to 100 of the Indians. Nobody doubted it. Mackenzie was the most efficient Indian fighter the army had. He was graduated from West Point in

The city of San Angelo owns Fort Concho now. Most of the buildings have been restored.

1862 as a second lieutenant and he had risen to the temporary rank of brigadier general by the end of the Civil War three years later.

The barracks at Fort Concho were crowded when Mackenzie and the 4th Cavalry came here after the Red River War. The 10th Cavalry was here, too. The post had been built to accommodate eight companies. There were 14 companies here for several months, until April of 1875 when Colonel William Shafter took several hundred cavalrymen and infantrymen out on an expedition to learn more about the

Colonel William Shafter led an expedition from Fort Concho to survey the High Plains area, after the Comanches were subdued. The old silver mining town of Shafter, Shafter Lake and Shafter Canyon were named for this officer. He picked up the nickname "Pecos Bill" during his time here.

plains. Most people had always assumed the High Plain was barren and waterless. Mackenzie had learned this was not entirely true. Shafter and his men set out with 65 wagons and 700 pack mules. They traveled some country whites had not seen before. They were gone for eight months. They discovered and charted many springs and ponds previously known only to the Indians. Shafter returned to report there was good pasturage as well as water on the South Plains. He predicted the frontier would advance 150 miles in the next two years.

Another expedition from Fort Concho was far less successful than Shafter's. Colonel Grierson sent Captain Nicholas Nolan and Company A of the 10th Cavalry out on July 4, 1877, to scout for hostile Indians. Nolan had Shafter's report on where the good water holes were. But he found out the water holes on the High Plain are not permanent. The weather had been dry since Shafter's expedition. Nolan and his cavalrymen met a party of buffalo hunters on the plain. The hunters were concerned about some Indians they said they had seen, so they asked if they could join Nolan's

A new school will be built to resemble the old Fort Concho hospital. It will be on the site this hospital occupied before it burned. Fort Concho is the scene of many San Angelo civic functions and celebrations. It is the most nearly complete frontier fort in Texas.

party. The hunters had as their guide the former Comanchero Jose Tafoya. They all spent the next several days searching for water.

Cedar Lake was dry. Several other water holes Shafter had reported were dry or had only a little salty water in them. The hunters and some of Nolan's men struck out on their own. Nolan and the men still with him were reduced to drinking their horses' urine and the blood of dying horses before they found water at Double Lake. They had been without water for 86 hours. Four soldiers, one civilian, 23 horses and four mules had died.

Some people blamed Nolan for the disaster. No action was taken against him, but four troopers were charged with desertion because they struck out on their own. They were convicted by a court martial and sentenced to short terms in the post stockade.

The black soldiers of the 9th and 10th Cavalry and the 24th and 25th Infantry were referred to by the Indians as "Buffalo soldiers," supposedly because their hair and complexion reminded the Indians of the buffalo. There was nothing uncomplimentary in the term. The Indians had a lot of respect for the buffalo and they learned to respect the buffalo soldiers. The troopers were proud to be called buffalo soldiers.

The civilians on the frontier had less respect for the black soldiers. Those around Fort Concho referred to the black troopers as "Grierson's brunettes." The civilians around Fort Concho were not a conspicuously respectable lot, themselves.

A trader named Bart DeWitt started a store across the river from the fort about 1870. A settlement developed as the opportunity for making money off the military drew to the Concho River the folks this opportunity usually drew. They were gamblers, saloon keepers, prostitutes, buffalo hunters and outlaws of all degrees. Cowmen driving stock along the Goodnight-Loving Trail also stopped at the settlement. J. Evetts Haley says there were 100 murders within three years in the bawdy town that became San Angelo. The story is that Bart DeWitt gave the settlement the name Santa Angela as a tribute to his wife's sister. People found San Angela easier to say. The Post Office Department changed it from San Angela to San Angelo.

The frontier defense line in the 1870s and '80s ran from Fort Duncan on the Rio Grande, to Fort Clark, to Fort Terrett, to Fort McKavett, to Fort Concho, to Fort Griffin to Fort Richardson. The forts farther west (Stockton, Davis and Bliss) were

mainly to protect the mail and stage line. Fort Concho was the halfway point on the frontier defense line and near the point where the main cross-country stage line turned west. It was an important fort and a busy place.

Fort Concho played a major role in the final phase of the Indian wars in Texas. Congress passed a law in 1880 forbidding any reservation Indians to enter Texas at any time for any purpose. It is impossible to say how much impression this made on the Indians. But there were numerous farms and ranches and settlements by this time well to the west of the frontier defense line. The Army was still at war with Indians beyond Texas, but the war with the Texas Indians was about over.

The Army decided in 1889 there was no longer any need for Fort Concho. There was a final muster on the parade ground. The band played *The Girl I Left Behind Me* and the troops marched off, but not into the sunset. The first railroad had reached San Angelo in 1888. The troops marched to the depot and rode away on the Santa Fe.

The Indians called the U.S. Cavalry's black troopers "Buffalo Soldiers." The men of the 10th Cavalry gloried in the title. They put a buffalo on their regimental emblem.

FORT ELLIOTT

*State highway 152, 1 mile west
of Mobeetie, Wheeler County.*

This was the only fort built to guard the border with Oklahoma; the only fort built in the Texas Panhandle. It was established after the Army forced the last tribes of Plains Indians onto the reservations in what was still called Indian Territory, in 1875. It was established to make sure the Indians did not stray back out onto the Panhandle plains.

The post was established originally on the North Fork of the Red River in February of 1875 and called the Cantonment on the North Fork of the Red River. It was moved closer to the headwaters of Sweetwater Creek in June of the same year and called New Cantonment until February of 1876 when the name was changed to Fort Elliott, in memory of Major Joel Elliott. He was a cavalry officer killed in a battle with Indians in the Indian Territory in 1868.

The first commanding officer at Fort Elliott was Major Henry Bankhead of the 4th Cavalry. A buffalo hunter was camped on Sweetwater Creek when the troops arrived to establish the post. The hunter reported that the sutlers had the saloon set up and open for business in less than half an hour. He was impressed.

The buildings at Fort Elliott were all frame. The materials were hauled in by wagon from Dodge City, Kansas. There were barracks for six companies of soldiers, four stables and houses for 13 officers by 1876. An English writer named Nugent Townsend visited here in 1879 and wrote that the frontier forts were pleasant oases in the cultural desert. He would have been even more impressed if he had come in 1889. The post had an ice machine by then.

All the supplies except hay and firewood had to be hauled 184 miles from Dodge City in the beginning. But as settlers moved in it became possible for the post to buy

There is nothing but a state marker at the site of Fort Elliott. The buildings were sold off and moved away. This is supposed to be the original Fort Elliott flagpole, outside the original Wheeler County Courthouse in old Mobeetie.

some foods and supplies locally. The post bakery sold bread to the settlers. There was a telegraph connection to Fort Sill, by 1879.

The troops stationed here went out on patrols for about a week at a time, looking for rustlers and Indians. The reservation Indians could get permission to hunt on the Texas plains until 1880 when Congress barred them from Texas.

The government leased the land here from 1875 until 1889 and then bought part of it just months before the fort was closed and abandoned in October of 1890. There was an auction in March of 1900. The buildings were sold to individuals for a total of $2348. The flagpole went for $7.50. The land was sold six years later for $11,000. The border with Oklahoma has been unprotected ever since.

The officers of Fort Elliott put on their best
uniforms to pose for this picture for a
visiting English writer in 1879.

FORT SAM HOUSTON

New Braunfels Avenue, northeast San Antonio, Bexar County.

The Army started building the arsenal that still stands on South Flores Street in San Antonio in 1859. Work was interrupted by the Civil War and resumed after the end of the war. The rest of the Army headquarters' business in San Antonio was conducted in rented quarters until 1879.

The Army had moved Texas headquarters to Austin once for a brief period and to Corpus Christi on another occasion. The people of San Antonio were anxious to keep

The Indian wars were about finished when the Army started building Fort Sam Houston. But the arrangement of the original buildings here more nearly resembles the standard conception of a fort than was the case at the posts on the Indian frontier. The stone buildings form a quadrangle with a stone clock and watch tower in the center. Fort Sam Houston is open to visitors all the time. The base is headquarters for the 5th Army. The Brooke Army Medical Center is here.

the headquarters here. The city first offered free land in 1846 but the Army never acted on that offer. The city started donating land for a permanent base in 1870 and made additional donations adding up to a total of 93 acres by 1874.

The Army was not sure what it wanted. Secretary of War William Belknap, General William Sherman and General Philip Sheridan all thought the spreading network of railroads would make it unnecessary to have a big central supply base in Texas. President Grant sided with San Antonio and General Sheridan eventually changed his mind. The Army finally let a contract for a fort on the donated site in 1876. The first stone buildings forming the quadrangle were completed in 1879 and the Army quartermaster depot moved from the Alamo to the new post. It was called the Post of San Antonio until 1890 when the Army named it for General Sam Houston.

Leonard Wood and Theodore Roosevelt recruited some of their Rough Riders for

The commanding general of the 5th Army
lives in this house. It is often called the
Pershing House because General John J.
Pershing was living here when he was
named to head the American Expeditionary
Force in Europe in World War I. The house
at No. 6 Staff Post Road was built in 1881.

the Spanish American War in this part of Texas. The Rough Riders were trained and outfitted at Fort Sam Houston and they left here for Cuba on May 30, 1898.

This was the biggest military base in the country by the early 1900s.

Lieutenant Benjamin Foulois made the first military airplane flight from the parade ground at Fort Sam Houston in 1910. He had learned a little about flying by talking and corresponding with the Wright Brothers. That experiment on the parade ground was the beginning of the Army Air Corps. It put Benjamin Foulois on his way to the job of commanding it. And it made San Antonio the home of the Air Force.

General John J. Pershing was commanding officer at Fort Sam Houston when we entered World War I in 1917. Fort Sam Houston and an annex called Camp Travis trained more than 200,000 men for the war. Leon Springs Military Reservation and Camp Bullis were established nearby to train officers.

Dwight Eisenhower, Arthur MacArthur, Douglas MacArthur, Carl Spaatz, Walter Krueger and Courtney Hodges all were stationed at Fort Sam Houston at various times. Eisenhower was here when he got his first star.

The Brooke Army Medical Center was established here in 1934. It was named for Brigadier General Roger Brooke. He was a distinguished Army medical officer and commander of the base hospital at Fort Sam Houston from 1928 to 1933.

Part of the site of Fort Pena Colorado is a county park with a small lake.

FORT PENA COLORADO

4 miles southwest of Marathon, Grewster County.

This cavalry post was established in March of 1880 when the Apaches were on the warpath. It is older than the nearby town of Marathon. The town developed after the railroad came in 1882. The military post was abandoned in February of 1893. No buildings survive. The site is now a county park with a small lake.

The only reminder that there was a military
post here is this marker.

FORT HANCOCK

State Highway 20,
Fort Hancock, Hudspeth
County.

This cavalry post was established in 1881. It guarded the border and the road between El Paso and San Antonio. The post originally was called Camp Rice and then named for General Winfield Scott Hancock. The Army turned the land over to the Interior Department when the fort was closed in 1895. It is now privately owned.

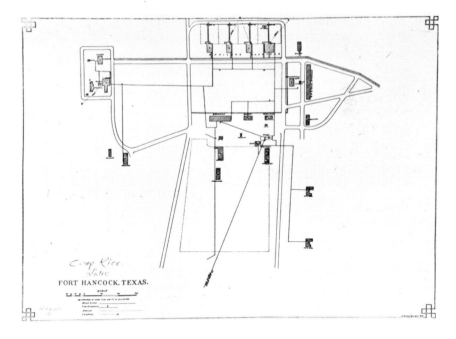

This is the original plan for the cavalry post first called Camp Rice. The camp was renamed for General Winfield Scott Hancock right after Hancock lost the 1880 presidential election to James Garfield.

Cotton grows today where the cavalry once paraded. The only reminders of the military history of this site are two markers. The one of the right is the original stone carved when the post was established as Camp Rice. The other is a memorial incorporating some fragments of the fort buildings, built by a local women's club.

Apache reservations had been established in New Mexico by the 1870s and many Apaches were living on the reservations but they were not all happy about it. A chief of the Mimbres Apache band named Victorio strayed off the reservations several times before 1879 when he recruited a couple hundred other Apaches and set out on a campaign against settlers, travelers and the Army. He fought off pursuing posses and soldiers in New Mexico, Mexico and Texas.

Colonel Benjamin Grierson was at Fort Concho with his 10th Cavalry when he got orders to end Victorio's rampage. Grierson moved west with six companies of the

Chief Victorio led a band of Apaches on a rampage that left an estimated 2000 people dead in Mexico, New Mexico and far west Texas in 1879 and 1880. His tactics were cited for years as models for guerrilla warfare.

10th Cavalry and six companies of infantry. They traveled hundreds of miles and tangled with the Apaches several times. But Victorio could not be cornered. He would lead his band across the river into Mexico when he came up against a force he couldn't handle. The Apaches were killing and plundering in Mexico, too, and Mexican troops got on their trail.

Colonel Grierson happened to be back at Fort Concho writing reports when he learned that a Mexican force led by Governor Juaquin Terrazas of Chihuahua had finally cornered the Apache band in the Tres Castillos Mountains and killed Victorio and most of his warriors on October 15, 1880.

Grierson was based at Fort Davis during part of the campaign against Victorio. He also established outposts at Camp Elizabeth, on the road between Fort Concho and Fort Stockton, and at a water hole he named Grierson Springs. Colonel Grierson and the 10th Cavalry were transferred from Fort Concho to Fort Davis in 1882. The 9th Cavalry had been transferred to New Mexico and then to Kansas in 1881. The 10th moved from Fort Davis to Arizona, in 1885. Geronimo's Apaches were still to be overcome there. But Texans finally had control over all the territory they claimed, thanks to the U.S. Army.

Benjamin Grierson led the U.S. troops in their campaign against the Apache band led by Chief Victorio. Grierson had risen to the temporary rank of major general in the Union army during the Civil War. He was appointed a colonel in the regular Army after the war and given responsibility for recruiting and organizing the 10th Cavalry. He commanded the 10th for 22 years.

**Fort Crockett
Fort San Jacinto
Fort Travis**

LATER FORTS

FORT CROCKETT

Seawall Boulevard, between 45th and 53rd streets, Galveston, Galveston County.

The Army bought the land and started building this fort in 1897. It was intended for coastal defense but the post was used first as a staging area for troops being shipped to Cuba for the Spanish American War in 1898. The fort was named for the Alamo hero Davy Crockett.

Fort Crockett suffered some damage in the 1900 hurricane. The seawall Galveston built after the storm was extended by the federal government in 1906 to protect the site of the fort. There was little going on at Fort Crockett between 1900 and 1911 when the Army started moving troops around to cope with disorders on the Mexican border. Three thousand soldiers and several hundred marines learned how to handle heavy artillery here during World War I.

The fort was expanded during World War II. Twenty-five hundred men were stationed here. They held firing drills on the 12-inch guns without notifying residents until Galvestonians' complaints convinced them it wouldn't cost anything extra to give a little notice. The concussion often broke windows.

The government used the fort as a recreation area and housed Coast Guard personnel here for a period of time after World War II. But it was plain there was

Gunners were trained for the Army and the
Marine Corps at Fort Crockett during World
War I.

no longer any need for a coastal artillery base in Galveston. The Army sold part of the Fort Crockett property in the 1960s for commercial development. Part of it was transferred to other public agencies and the government kept several buildings for the National Marine Fisheries Service. George Mitchell's Hotel San Luis now stands on part of the fort site.

The San Luis Hotel now occupies this part of the site of Fort Crockett. The casemates built for the fort's 12-inch guns are incorporated in the hotel building.

FORT SAN JACINTO

*Eastern end of Seawall
Boulevard, Galveston,
Galveston County.*

The Army built this coastal artillery base in 1898 on what had been the site of the first fort established by the Republic of Texas in 1836. The federal fort here at the eastern tip of Galveston Island shared with Fort Travis the responsibility for protecting the entrance to the Galveston and Houston channels.

Both channel forts were closed after World War II. The government still owns the site of Fort San Jacinto but little remains of the fort.

Remains of a gun position at what was Fort San Jacinto on the eastern tip of Galveston Island.

FORT TRAVIS

Eastern tip of Bolivar Peninsula off State Highway 87, Galveston County.

This was a coastal artillery post designed to help protect the entrance to the Galveston and Houston ship channels. There were more big guns on the other side of the entrance, at Fort San Jacinto on the eastern tip of Galveston Island.

The Army started building this base in 1898. A seawall was built to protect it after the great storm of 1900. The guns were ready and the gunners watchful throughout World War I and World War II. But no enemy ship ever tried to intrude. The guns here were fired only for practice.

The base was dismantled after World War II. The property is now a county park.

The western tip of Bolivar Peninsula, at the entrance to Galveston Harbor, has a long military history. The filibuster James Long had a camp here when Texas was still Spanish. There were Confederate fortifications here during the Civil War. Substantial gun platforms built by the U.S. Army in the 1890s and early 1900s still stand on the site that is now a county park.

The Galveston Island gambling syndicates hid some of their gambling equipment here at old Fort Travis during Attorney General Will Wilson's crackdown in the late 1950s. Five hundred and fifty slot machines were found and seized here.

APPENDIX

The building of federal forts to protect Texas ended with the coastal artillery bases at Galveston, except for a few cavalry posts set up to deal with the Mexican bandits and revolutionaries in the early 1900s. But the Army has kept major units in Texas continuously since the end of the Civil War, as what had been a frontier in need of protection became a convenient, hospitable and roomy place to base and train troops.

The later bases and training camps, federal posts not mentioned previously and other establishments in Texas designated as forts, military camps or presidios are listed here.

SPANISH

The Alamo is the most famous military post in Texas history.

The Alamo

The Mission San Antonio de Valero was established by the Spanish on the San Antonio River in 1718 and moved to the present site in 1724. The mission was closed in 1793.

The compound was occupied by Spanish troops resisting the Mexican campaign for independence. Those troops came from Alamo del Parras, Couhuila. This probably is why the old compound came to be called the Alamo, years after it had ceased to be a mission. But it is also possible that the old mission got its informal name from the cottonwood trees in the neighborhood. *Alamo* is the Spanish word for cottonwood.

Mexican troops occupied the Alamo off and on after the Mexican revolution succeeded in 1821. They were besieged by Texas revolutionaries and forced to surrender in December, 1835. The Texans held the town and the old mission until a Mexican army led by President Antonio Lopez de Santa Anna arrived and took the town February 23, 1836. The Mexicans overwhelmed the Texas garrison commanded by William Barret Travis and reclaimed the Alamo March 6, 1836. All the defenders were killed. The mission compound was in ruins. The walls and most of the buildings were demolished as San Antonio grew. The government of the Republic deeded the mission chapel to the Catholic Church in 1846. But U.S. troops took it over after the annexation and used it off and on until almost 1880.

The state of Texas finally bought the chapel in 1883 and then bought the surviving barracks building next door in 1905. Clara Driscoll and the Daughters of the Republic of Texas engineered the purchase and the Daughters have had custody of the surviving properties ever since. There is a museum in the barracks building at the Alamo Plaza in downtown San Antonio. The museum and the chapel are open to visitors every day.

Fort Anahuac

Established in 1821, this fort was the scene of an early clash between colonists and Mexican officials in 1832. There is a state marker in the county park at Anahuac, Chambers County.

Fort Chambers

Another name for Fort Anahuac.

Fort Lipantitlan

Earthworks engineered in 1728 and abandoned in 1813. Occupied by Mexican troops in 1831. There is a state marker in a small county park at the site, off Farm Road 3088, 20 miles northwest of Corpus Christi, Nueces County.

Presidio del Norte

Adobe buildings erected in 1759 at or near the present site of Fort Leaton on the Rio Grande at the Concho, 3 miles below the present town of Presidio.

Presidio de Nuestra Senora de los Dolores de los Tejas

Built in 1716 to protect the Mission San Francisco de los Tejas. Abandoned in 1729. There is a state marker at the site, 6 miles south of Douglas, Nacogdoches County.

Presidio de San Agustin de Ahumada (El Orcoquisac)

Established in 1756 to protect the Franciscans' Mission Nuestra Senora de la Luz. Abandoned in 1772. There is a state marker ¼-mile east of the Trinity River bridge, I-10, Chambers County.

Presidio La Bahia

The proper name is Presidio Nuestra Senora de Loreto. It protected Mission Nuestra Senora del Espiritu Santo de Zuniga, on Matagorda Bay; established in 1722 and moved to present site in 1749. Texans seized it from the Mexicans in October, 1835. Texas troops commanded by Colonel James Fannin were captured by Mexicans near here March 20, 1836, and executed here March 27, 1836. It has been restored and is the property of the Catholic Church. Highway 77A-183, south of Goliad, Goliad County.

Presidio Santa Cruz

A small stockade post built in 1772 on the road between San Antonio and La Bahia (Goliad), on Cibolo Creek.

Presidio San Francisco Xavier

Established in 1748 to protect the Franciscans' San Xavier missions, near the junction of Brushy Creek and San Gabriel River. The garrison later moved to the San Saba Presidio. There is a state marker 8 miles west of Rockdale, on Farm Road 908, Milam County.

Presidio San Luis de las Amarillas de San Saba

Also called San Saba Presidio, it was built in 1757 to protect the Mission San Saba de la Santa Cruz. Abandoned in 1768, the ruins were partially rebuilt in 1936. There is a marker at the site, 1 mile west of Menard on State Highway 29.

FRENCH

Champ d'Aisle

Some of Napoleon Bonaparte's exiled supporters established this settlement in 1817 on the Trinity River. They apparently meant it to be a base for a Bonaparte revival but they fled to New Orleans when they heard that a Spanish army was on the way from Mexico to evict them. There is a state marker on U.S. 90 near the east bank of the Trinity River, Liberty County.

Fort St. Louis

Established in 1685 by LaSalle after he apparently lost his way and landed on the Texas coast while looking for the mouth of the Mississippi. It is believed to have been 13 miles southeast of present town of Inez. There is a state marker on U.S. 59 at Farm Road 444, Inez, Victoria County.

Spanish Fort

An outpost established on the Red River in 1719 where the French traded with the Indians. The Spanish attacked this camp in 1759 and they left some equipment behind when they were driven off. The Spanish artifacts caused later settlers to think there had been a Spanish fort here. There is a state marker on Farm Road 103 in the settlement of Spanish Fort, Montague County.

REPUBLIC OF TEXAS

Bird's Fort

A Texas Ranger post established in 1841 by Jonathan Bird. It became the village of Birdville and Birdville became the first county seat of Tarrant County. There is a state marker 7 miles north of Arlington, off State Highway 183.

Fort Boggy

A Texas Ranger post established in 1840. There is a state marker 5 miles south of Centerville, Leon County.

Fort Burleson

A temporary Texas Ranger camp in 1839 on the Brazos River, Falls County.

Camp Cazneau

Established in 1841, President Mirabeau Lamar's Santa Fe Expedition mustered here for the march to New Mexico. The camp was adjacent to Kenney's Fort, Williamson County.

Camp Coleman

A Texas Ranger post established in 1836. Log cabins protected by a stockade. Named for the commanding officer, Captain Robert Coleman. There is a state marker 2 miles east of Austin city limits, on Farm Road 969, Travis County.

Fort Defiance

The name Colonel James Fannin and his garrison gave the Presidio La Bahia while they were occupying it in 1836. Goliad County.

Fort Fisher

A Texas Ranger post established on the Brazos River in 1837. A replica was built in 1968 as part of the Texas Ranger Museum. I-35 at the Brazos, Waco, McLennan County.

Fort Houston

A blockhouse and log cabins built in 1836 and abandoned in 1841 or 1842. There is a state marker at the intersection of U.S. 79 and Farm Road 1990, 2 miles south of Palestine, Anderson County.

Camp Independence

Established in 1836. Part of the Texas army camped here after the battle of San Jacinto. General Felix Huston and General Albert Sidney Johnston fought a duel here when Huston resisted Johnston's attempt to relieve him. Abandoned in 1837. There is a state marker 1 mile off Farm Road 234, 5 miles southwest of Edna, Jackson County.

Fort Johnson

Established in 1840, it was the first of a chain of forts proposed to protect the military road from the Red River to Austin. There is a state marker 4 miles north of Pottsboro on Farm Road 120, Grayson County.

Little River Fort

A Texas Ranger post established in 1836. Sometimes called Fort Griffin, it consisted of log cabins surrounded by a stockade. There is a state marker 5 miles southeast of Belton, on Farm Road 436, Bell County.

Fort Milam

A Texas Ranger post established in 1836 to protect settlers at Sarahville de Viesca, in the Sterling Robertson Colony. There is a state marker west of Farm Road 2027, just below the Falls of the Brazos, Falls County.

Fort Smith

A Texas Ranger outpost established in 1839 and named for Major Thomas Smith. There is a state marker 8 miles east of Itasca, on Farm Road 934, Hill County.

Fort Travis

The first fort established by the Republic, in 1836, to protect the entrance to Galveston Harbor.

FEDERAL

Camp Austin

Also called Post of Austin. The Army had a temporary military depot on the Colorado River in the capital between 1848 and 1852. The city was also occupied after the Civil War by General George Custer and units of the 6th Cavalry. The Custers lived in the building that had housed the State Blind Asylum. The building is now the University of Texas Visitors' Center.

Camp Barkeley

Established in 1940. The 45th and 90th divisions trained here for World War II. It was one of the biggest bases in Texas at the time but it was declared surplus in 1945. Part of it is now a National Guard base, 8 miles southwest of Abilene, on Farm Road 1235, Taylor County.

Camp Blake

A temporary camp on the road between San Antonio and El Paso in Val Verde County, used by travelers in the 1840s.

General George Custer and his family lived in this house while at Camp Austin after the Civil War. It is now the University of Texas Visitors' Center.

Camp Bowie

Established in two locations: Fort Worth in World War I and Brownwood in World War II. The 36th Division trained at both locations. Nothing remains of the original Camp Bowie, on Camp Bowie Boulevard in Fort Worth. The second Camp Bowie, in Brownwood, Brown County, is now an industrial park.

The 36th Division trained at both locations of Camp Bowie. Nothing remains of this first camp, used during World War I, on Camp Bowie Boulevard in Fort Worth.

Camp Bullis

Established in 1917, it served as a maneuver area and target range for troops training at Fort Sam Houston and Camp Travis during World War I. Named for John L. Bullis, leader of the Seminole Indian scouts during the Indian wars. This is a subpost of Fort Sam Houston and still active. Off I-10 West, northwest of San Antonio, Bexar County.

Camp Cabell

A temporary camp, occupied in 1898 by the 2nd Texas Volunteer Infantry during the Spanish-American War; Dallas, Dallas County.

Camp Casa Blanca

Also called Camp Merrill, it was established in 1852 as a temporary subpost of Fort Merrill, on the Nueces River. There is a state marker on State Highway 359, at Sandia, Jim Wells County.

Camp Charlotte

A temporary outpost established in 1853 on the El Paso Mail Road on the Middle Concho River, Irion County.

Camp Corpus Christi

Also called Post of Corpus Christi, it was the temporary headquarters of the Department of Texas in the 1850s.

Camp Elizabeth

A temporary camp established in 1853, it was later an outpost of Fort Concho in the 1870s. There is a state marker on U.S. 87, 9 miles northwest of Sterling City, Sterling County.

Camp Fannin

Established in 1942 as an infantry training base and detention camp for German prisoners of war during World War II. Closed in 1946, it is now the University of Texas Health Center, 10 miles northeast of Tyler, on U.S. 271, Smith County.

Camp Grierson

An outpost of Fort Concho, established by Colonel Benjamin Grierson in 1878 on Live Oak Creek, Reagan County.

Camp Harney

A temporary post established in 1851, it was named for Colonel William Harney. Zapata County.

Camp Helena

A cavalry post established during the period of border troubles in 1910. Permanent buildings were never occupied by the soldiers who were transferred about the time the adobe buildings were completed. The buildings are in good condition and used by park employees. Castolon, on the Rio Grande, Big Bend National Park, Brewster County.

Camp Holland

A supply base for troops patrolling the Mexican border, established in 1918 and abandoned in 1920, 12 miles west of Valentine, Jeff Davis County.

One of the adobe buildings erected at
Camp Helena in 1910 is now a park
ranger station and store in Big Bend
National Park on the Rio Grande.

Fort Hood has been the home of Patton's famed 2nd Armored Division since World War II. It was used during the war in Vietnam as a basic training post.

Fort Hood

Established in 1942 to train soldiers in techniques for destroying enemy tanks. Named for Confederate General John Bell Hood, it is the present home of the 2nd Armored Division and the 1st Cavalry Division. Located in Bell and Coryell counties, the main entrance is on U.S. 190 near Killeen.

Camp Hulen

Originally a National Guard camp, established in 1940 and named for General John Hulen of the Texas National Guard. It served as a training camp for anti-aircraft crews in World War II and was closed in 1946. Palacious, Matagorda County.

Fort Ives

A temporary outpost of Camp Verde in 1859, located on Turtle Creek in eastern Kerr County.

Post of Jefferson

No fort was built in this East Texas river town, but troops were stationed here for a period after the Civil War. The Army rented buildings in town for the commissary and quartermaster stores. The troops lived in tents in a camp on the southwestern outskirts of Jefferson, Marion County.

Camp Joseph E. Johnston

A temporary post on the North Concho River, occupied March to November, 1853. Northwest Tom Green County.

Camp Logan

Established in 1917 to train National Guard units for World War I. No buildings survive. Memorial Park now occupies most of the site, on Memorial Drive, Houston, Harris County.

Camp MacArthur

A training camp established in 1917 for National Guard units in World War I. Named for Douglas MacArthur's father, General Arthur MacArthur, it was closed in 1918. There is a state marker at 3716 North 19th Street, Waco, McLennan County.

Camp Maxey

An infantry training camp named for Confederate General Samuel Bell Maxey. Established in 1942, it was closed 1945. 10 miles north of Paris, Lamar County.

Camp Melvin

A temporary outpost established in 1868 on the Pecos River, Crockett County.

Camp Nowlin

A temporary camp, set up in 1859 by troops escorting Indians from the Brazos Reservation to Oklahoma Territory, on Little Wichita River, Archer County.

Fort D.A. Russell

Cavalry headquarters when units of the 3rd, 6th, 8th, 14th and 15th Cavalry Regiments were patrolling the border. Established in 1920 and occupied until 1945, it was named for an officer killed in the Mexican War. Many buildings are still standing off U.S. 67 on the south side of Marfa, Presidio County.

Camp Sabinal

A temporary cavalry outpost established in 1856 on the San Antonio-El Paso Road at the Sabinal River and used by the 2nd Cavalry for about 6 months. It was used later by Texas Rangers. There is a state marker on U.S. 90, 1 mile west of Sabinal, Uvalde County.

Camp San Felipe

Established in 1857 as an outpost of Fort Clark at Del Rio in Val Verde County.

Camp Stanley

Originally established as an outpost of the San Antonio Arsenal. Now a subpost of Camp Bullis, at Leon Springs, Bexar County.

Camp Swift

Established in 1942 to train infantry units for World War II. It was named for General Eben Swift, commander of the 82nd Division in World War I, and was closed in 1947. The site is now occupied by a National Guard base, a federal prison and a cancer research center. Off State Highway 95, north of Bastrop, Bastrop County.

Camp Travis

A temporary camp established in 1917 adjacent to Fort Sam Houston where 100,000 troops trained for World War I. It was later incorporated into Fort Sam Houston, San Antonio, Bexar County.

Camp Van Camp

A temporary camp established in 1859, and named for Lieutenant Cornelius Van Camp of the 2nd Cavalry after he was killed in a fight with Indians. There is a state marker on State Highway 251, at the southern edge of Newcastle, Young County.

Camp Wallace

Established in 1941 to train anti-aircraft crews for World War II. It was named for Colonel Elmer Wallace, killed in France in World War I. Camp Wallace was transferred to the navy in 1944 and it was also one of the bases where German prisoners of war were held. The frame buildings were sold after the base was closed in 1946. Part of the site is now a park. State Highway 6, south of Hitchcock, Galveston County.

Camp Wichita

A temporary cavalry outpost in the 1870s on the military road between the Red River and Fort Richardson, Jack County.

Fort Wolters

A National Guard training camp established in 1925. It was originally called Camp Wolters for General Joseph Wolters. The U.S. Army used it as infantry training base in World War II. It was closed after the war. The base was reactivated in 1951 as a training center for Air Force helicopter crews. The Air Force left in 1956 and the Army started training helicopter crews here. This was the principal training base for helicopter crews during the war in Vietnam. It was closed in 1973. Most of the buildings are still standing. Part of the site is an industrial park, part is a college campus and part is a park. Off U.S. 180, east of Mineral Wells, in Parker County.

CONFEDERATE

Camp Breckenridge

A Frontier Regiment post established in 1862. There is a state marker on the courthouse grounds, Breckenridge, Stephens County.

Camp Clark

Established by and named for Governor Edward Clark in 1861, it was used as a training base for the 4th Texas Infantry and the 36th Texas Cavalry during the Civil War. There is a state marker in City Park, Staples, Guadalupe County.

Camp Collier

One of the Frontier Regiment posts, it was established in 1862 on Clear Creek. There is a state marker on the courthouse grounds, Brownwood, Brown County.

Camp Cureton

One of the Frontier Regiment posts, established in 1862 and named for Captain Jack Cureton. It was located on the West Fork of the Trinity River. There is a state marker on the courthouse grounds, Archer City, Archer County.

Camp Davis

One of the Frontier Regiment posts, established in 1862 and named for Captain H.T. Davis. It was located at the junction of White Oak Creek and Pedernales River, Gillespie County.

Camp Dix

A Frontier Regiment camp, named for Captain J.J. Dix, established in 1862 on the Frio River, Uvalde County.

Camp Drum

A temporary camp established in 1862 on the Rio Grande at Zapata, Zapata County.

Fort Esperanza

Established in 1863 as part of the Texas coastal defense system during the Civil War. Located near the lighthouse on Matagorda Island at what was then called Saluria. The site was later occupied by the Matagorda Air Force Base. It is now a state park. The outlines of the trenches are still visible from the air.

Camp Ford

A stockade established in 1862 as a prison camp for captured Union soldiers. Six thousand prisoners were here at one time. Union occupation troops destroyed the camp after the war. There is a state marker in a roadside park on U.S. 271, 4 miles northeast of Tyler, Smith County.

Fort Green

Established in 1861 as part of the Texas coastal defense system during the Civil War on the same site as the later, federal, Fort Travis, on the west end of Bolivar Peninsula, Galveston County.

Fort Griffin

Another name for Fort Sabine established in 1861 in Jefferson County.

Camp Groce

A detention camp for Union prisoners, established in 1861 at Liendo Plantation, 3½ miles east of Hempstead, Waller County.

Camp Kenny

One of the Frontier Regiment posts during the Civil War, established in 1861, and used by Texas Rangers during the 1870s. It was located on Gonzales Creek, southern Stephens County.

Camp Liendo

Another name for Camp Groce. General George Custer and the 6th U.S. Cavalry camped here enroute to Austin to take up occupation duties in 1865.

Camp Llano

One of the Frontier Regiment outposts, established in 1862 at the junction of Rock Creek and the Llano River, Mason County.

Fort Manhassett

Established in 1863 as part of the Texas coastal defense system during the Civil War, it consisted of earthworks with 10 cannon and 500 men. There is a state marker 6½ miles west of Sabine Pass, on State Highway 87, Jefferson County.

This replica of Fort Fisher was built in 1968 as part of the Texas Ranger Museum. Located in Waco, it is open to the public.

Camp McMillan

One of the Frontier Regiment outposts, established in 1862 and named for Captain N.D. McMillan. There is a state marker on the courthouse grounds, San Saba, San Saba County.

Camp Montel

One of the Frontier Regiment outposts during the Civil War, established in 1862 on Seco Creek and named for Captain Charles de Montel. There is a state marker on the courthouse grounds, Bandera, Bandera County.

Camp Nueces

One of the Frontier Regiment outposts during the Civil War, established in 1862 and commanded by Captain J.J. Dix, on the Nueces River, Uvalde County.

Camp Pecan

A Frontier Regiment camp during the Civil War. Established on Pecan Bayou in 1862 and commanded by Captain T.M. Collier. Callahan County.

Camp Rabb

A Frontier Regiment post established in 1862 on Elm Creek and commanded by Captain Thomas Rabb. Maverick County.

Fort Sabine

Built in 1861, it consisted of earthworks reinforced with steel rails from the rail line that ran between Beaumont and Orange. Lieutenant Dick Dowling and a small garrison broke up and captured part of a Union invasion force here September 8, 1863. The U.S. Army had a coastal artillery post on the same site in World War II. It is now a county park, off State Highway 87, just south of Sabine Pass, Jefferson County.

Camp San Saba

One of the Frontier Regiment outposts during the Civil War, commanded by Captain N.D. McMillan. Established in 1862 on the San Saba River. There is a state marker on U.S. 87, 10 miles south of Brady, McCulloch County.

Camp Waul

Established in 1862 as a training camp for Waul's Legion, organized and led by Gonzales County planter Thomas Waul. Near Brenham, Washington County.

MEXICAN

Fort Tenoxtitlan

Established in 1830 on the Brazos River at Old San Antonio Road crossing, near Caldwell, Burleson County. It was abandoned in 1832 and there is now a state marker 14 miles northeast of Caldwell, off Farm Road 1362.

Fort Teran

Established in 1831 on Shawnee Creek, Tyler County, it was commanded by Colonel Peter Ellis Bean. When Bean and the garrison were transferred to Nacogdoches in 1832 the fort was closed. There is a state marker 11 miles northeast of Chester, off Farm Road 1745.

Fort Velasco

Established in 1830. Anglo settlers won a skirmish with Mexican troops here June 26, 1832. Santa Anna signed the treaty recognizing Texas independence here May 14, 1836. A Confederate fort on the same site protected the mouth of the Brazos during the Civil War. There is a state marker 5 miles east of Freeport on Farm Road 523, Brazoria County.

2000 FEET SOUTH
SITE OF

FORT TENOXTITLAN

ESTABLISHED BY THE MEXICAN GOVERN-
MENT IN JULY, 1830, IN AN ATTEMPT
TO STEM ANGLO-AMERICAN SETTLEMENT ·
NAMED IN HONOR OF THE AZTEC
CAPITOL, NOW MEXICO CITY · ABANDONED
BY MEXICAN TROOPS IN 1832 · IN THE
TOWN WHICH GREW UP AFTER 1834
MANY PROMINENT TEXANS LIVED · THE
PLACE PASSED FROM THE MAP AFTER 1860

This marker was erected by the Texas
Centennial Commission in 1836 near the
site of Fort Tenoxtitlan on the Brazos River.
Established by the Mexican government in
1830, the fort was named in honor of the
Aztec capitol, now Mexico City.

STATE OF TEXAS

Fort Fitzhugh

A Texas Ranger post estabished in 1847 and commanded by Colonel William Fitzhugh. It was located 3 miles south of Gainesville, Cooke County.

Camp Mabry

Established in 1890 as a summer camp for the Texas Volunteer Guard that later became the National Guard. Named for Texas Adjutant General Woodford Mabry, it was used by the U.S. Army in World War I and World War II. Austin, Travis County.

Camp Montel

A Texas Volunteer Guard post established in 1870 by Captain Charles de Montel on the Nueces River in Uvalde County. The town of Montell grew up around this camp.

PRIVATE FORTS

Fort Bend

A stout log cabin built in 1821 by the earliest settlers on a bend of the Brazos. The city of Richmond developed around it and the county took its name from this fort. There is a state marker on the west bank of the Brazos between the eastbound and westbound bridges, U.S. 90A, Richmond, Fort Bend County.

Fort Blair

Built by C.C. Blair in 1861 to protect his family and neighbors from the Indians during the Civil War. There is a state marker on State Highway 16, Desdemona, Eastland County.

Fort Cibolo

Adobe structures built in the 1850s by rancher Milton Favor to protect his livestock, near Shafter, Presidio County.

Fort Cienaga

Built in the 1850s by rancher Milton Favor to protect his property and livestock, near Shafter, Presidio County.

Fort Inglish

A blockhouse and stockade built in 1837 by early settler Bailey Inglish on Powder Creek. A replica has been built and there is a state marker on Loop 205, Bonham, Fannin County.

Fort Lacy

A fortified home and trading post built in 1833 by Martin Lacy. There is a state marker 2 miles southwest of Alto, Cherokee County.

Fort Leaton

A fortified adobe trading post built by and named for Ben Leaton in 1846, it may be on a site occupied earlier by the Spanish Presidio del Norte. It has been rebuilt and is now a state park, 3 miles below Presidio on Farm Road 170, Presidio County.

Fort Leaton, a fortified adobe trading post, has been rebuilt and is now a state park near Presidio.

Fort Moritas

An adobe structure built in the 1850s by rancher Milton Favor to protect his land and livestock from the Apaches, near Shafter, Presidio County.

Fort Oldham

Built in 1836 by Major William Oldham for the protection of his family and neighbors. There is a state marker 2½ miles southwest of Cook's Point on Farm Road 1362, Burleson County.

Fort Parker

A stockade built in 1834 by Silas and James Parker. Five people were killed and five kidnapped during a Comanche raid here in May, 1836. One of those kidnapped was Cynthia Ann Parker. It has been rebuilt and is now a state park, 8 miles southwest of Mexia, off State Highway 14, Limestone County.

Fort Picketville

A family fort built in 1854, 2 miles north of Breckenridge, Stephens County.

Now rebuilt, Fort Parker was the scene of the Comanche kidnapping of Cynthia Ann Parker. She was the mother of Quanah Parker, the last Comanche war chief.

Fort Ramirez

A fortified ranch house built in 1813 by Eduardo Ramirez while Texas was still Spanish. There is a state marker off U.S. 281, 23 miles south of George West, Live Oak County.

Fort Sherman

A stockade built in 1838 by early settler W.B. Stout to protect his family and neighbors from the Indians, it is said to have been on Cypress Creek, Titus County.

Fort Spunky

A fortified trading post built in 1847 by George Barnard in southeast Hood County.

Fort Sullivan

A fortified trading post built in 1835 by A.W. Sullivan. There is a state marker 11 miles east of Maysfield, on a county road off U.S. 190, Milam County.

Kenny's Fort

A family stockade built in 1838 by Dr. Thomas Kenney. There is a state marker 2½ miles east of Round Rock, on State Highway 29, Williamson County.

Wood's Fort

The fortified residence of Zadock Woods, one of Stephen F. Austin's original 300 colonists, built in 1828. There is a state marker 1½ miles west of West Point on State Highway 7, Fayette County.

INDEX
Presidios, camps and forts in Texas

Alamo, The: 181
Anahuac, Fort: 182
Austin, Camp: 188
Barkeley, Camp: 188
Belknap, Fort: 53
Bend, Fort: 211
Bird's Fort: 185
Blair, Fort: 211
Blake, Camp: 188
Bliss, Fort: 27
Boggy, Fort: 185
Bowie, Camp: 190
Breckenridge, Camp: 202
Brown, Fort: 15
Bullis, Camp: 192
Burleson, Fort: 185
Cabell, Camp: 192
Casa Blanca, Fort: 192
Cazneau, Camp: 185
Chadbourne, Fort: 81
Champ d'Aisle: 184
Chambers, Fort: 182
Charlotte, Camp: 192
Cibolo, Camp: 211
Cienaga, Camp: 211
Clark, Camp: 202
Clark, Fort: 77
Coleman, Camp: 185
Collier, Camp: 202
Colorado, Camp: 96
Concho, Fort: 143
Cooper, Camp: 90
Corpus Christi, Camp: 193
Crockett, Fort: 169
Croghan, Fort: 41
Cureton, Camp: 202
Davis, Camp: 202
Davis, Fort: 83
D.A. Russell, Fort: 199
Defiance, Fort: 185
Dix, Camp: 203
Drum, Camp: 203
Duncan, Fort: 25
Elizabeth, Camp: 193
Elliot, Fort: 152
Esperanza, Fort: 203
Ewell, Fort: 76
Fannin, Camp: 193
Fisher, Fort: 186
Fitzhugh, Fort: 210
Ford, Camp: 203
Gates, Fort: 48
Graham, Fort: 42
Green, Fort: 203
Grierson, Camp: 193
Griffin, Fort (confederate): 204
Griffin, Fort (federal): 137
Groce, Camp: 204
Hancock, Fort: 163
Harney, Camp: 194
Helena, Camp: 194
Holland, Camp: 194
Hood, Fort: 197
Houston, Fort: 186
Hudson, Camp: 98
Hulen, Camp: 197
Independence, Camp: 186
Inge, Fort: 39
Inglish, Fort: 212
Ives, Fort: 197
Johnson, Fort: 186
Johnston, Camp: 75
Joseph E. Johnston, Camp: 198
Kenny, Camp: 204
Kenny's Fort: 217
Lacy, Fort: 212
Lancaster, Fort: 88
Leaton, Fort: 212

Liendo, Camp: 204
Little River Fort: 186
Lincoln, Fort: 47
Lipantitlan, Fort: 182
Llano, Camp: 204
Logan, Camp: 198
Mabry, Camp: 210
MacArthur, Camp: 198
Manhassett, Fort: 204
Martin Scott, Fort: 37
Mason, Fort: 58
Maxey, Camp: 198
McIntosh, Fort: 22
McKavett, Fort: 71
McMillan, Camp: 206
Melvin, Camp: 198
Merrill, Fort: 49
Milam, Fort: 187
Montel, Camp (Confederate): 206
Montel, Camp (State of Texas): 210
Moritas, Fort: 214
Nowlin, Camp: 199
Nueces, Camp: 206
Oldham, Fort: 214
Parker, Fort: 214
Pecan, Camp: 206
Pena Colorado, Fort: 161
Phantom Hill, Fort: 64
Picketville, Fort: 214
Post of San Elizario: 35
Post of Jefferson: 197
Presidio del Norte: 182
Presidio de Nuestra Senora
   de los Dolores de los Tejas: 182
Presidio de San Agustin
   de Ahumada (El Orcoquisac): 182
Presidio La Bahia: 183
Presidio Santa Cruz: 183
Presidio San Francisco Xavier: 183
Presidio San Luis de las Amarillas
   de San Saba: 183
Quitman, Fort: 99
Rabb, Camp: 206
Ramirez, Fort: 216
Richardson, Fort: 131
Ringgold, Fort: 19
Sabinal, Camp: 199
Sabine, Fort: 207
Sam Houston, Fort: 156
San Felipe, Camp: 199
San Jacinto, Fort: 173
San Saba, Camp: 207
Sherman, Fort: 216
Smith, Fort: 187
Spanish Fort: 184
Spunky, Fort: 216
Stanley, Camp: 199
St. Louis, Fort: 184
Stockton, Fort: 102
Sullivan, Fort: 217
Swift, Camp: 200
Tenoxtitlan, Fort: 208
Teran, Fort: 208
Terrett, Fort: 68
Travis, Camp: 200
Travis, Fort (federal): 174
Travis, Fort (republic): 187
Van Camp, Camp: 200
Velasco, Fort: 208
Verde, Camp: 94
Wallace, Camp: 200
Waul, Camp: 207
Wichita, Camp: 201
Wolters, Fort: 201
Wood, Camp: 97
Wood's Fort: 217
Worth, Fort: 44

ACKNOWLEDGEMENTS

The author and publisher are indebted to many individuals and institutions for advice and assistance. Special thanks to Jerry Sullivan, Leroy Williamson, Glen Mills and Susie Gonzalez of *Texas Parks & Wildlife*; Thomas Cutrer, Associate Director of the Texas State Historical Association; Tom Munnerlyn of State House Books in Austin; Bill Reaves and Linda Fink of *Texas Highways*; Doris Glasser and the staff of the Texas and Local History Room, Houston Public Library; the Fort Concho Museum and Library; Ralph Elder of the Eugene C. Barker Texas History Center at the University of Texas at Austin; Toni Harris of Austin, Dow Warren of Houston and Bob Nesbit of Galveston.

Publications recommended to readers wishing more information:

American Firearms: Van Rensselaer
Army Life on the Border: Marcy
Ben Holladay, The Stage Coach King: Frederick
Buffalo Soldiers, The: Leckie
Butterfield Overland Mail, The: Conkling and Conkling
Butterfield Overland Mail, The: Wright and Bynum
Fort Bliss: Metz
Fort Brown: Marcum
Fort Concho and the Texas Frontier: Haley
Fort Concho in 1877: Miles
Fort Griffin on the Texas Frontier: Rister
Fort Quitman: Cage
Fort Richardson, Outpost on the Texas Frontier: Whisenhunt
Fort Worth, A Frontier Triumph: Garrett
Forts and Treasure Trails of West Texas: Gibson
Forts of the West: Frazer
Frontier Defense in Texas, 1846-1860: Holden
Frontier Defense in Texas During the Civil War: Holden
Frontier Defense, 1865-1889: Holden
Frontier Forts of Texas: Simpson, Conger, Day,
    Frantz, Neighbors, Nunn, Procter and Winfrey
Handbook of Texas, The: Texas State Historical Association
History of Fort Elliot: Oswald
History of Fort Sam Houston: Handy

Indians of Texas, The: Newcomb
Lone Star: Fehrenbach
Musket, Sabre and Missile, A History of Fort Bliss: McMaster
Old Forts of the Southwest: Hart
Pioneer Posts of Texas: Toulouse and Toulouse
Republic of Texas, The, Its History and Annexation: Jones
Sharps Rifles and Spanish Mules, The San Antonio-El Paso Mail: Austerman
Spurs to Glory, The Story of the United States Cavalry: Merrill
Stagecoach Pioneers of the Southwest: Mullin
Story of Fort Davis: Scobee
Through Unexplored Texas: Parker

PHOTO CREDITS

The photographs for this book were taken by the author and his associates except for those listed below. The author and the publisher wish to express their gratitude and appreciation to these individuals, institutions and organizations for permitting the reproduction of photographs from their collections. Dow Warren of Houston has assembled a slide presentation that highlights several of the frontier forts; his photograph of Fort Griffin appears on the cover. Jerry Sullivan of *Texas Parks & Wildlife* offered advice and suggestions for locating historical photographs as did Toni Harris of Austin. Rich Hall of Houston took the photo of Ray Miller that appears on the back cover.

Bill Dennis, Jacksboro (Texas Parks & Wildlife collection): 135
Dow Warren: 81, 95 (bottom)
Fort Concho Museum: 143, 148
Fort Sill Museum: 126
Fort Union National Historic Site: *The Battle of Adobe Walls*
  by Nick Eggenhofer, 116
Kansas City Historical Society: 139
Harper's Magazine (Texas Parks & Wildlife collection):
  Fort Lancaster 1860, 88
Institute of Texan Cultures: 115
Metropolitan Research Center, Houston Public Library: 3, 9, 63, 77, 90, 112,
  119, 129, 170, 190
National Archives: 12, 19, 27, 60, 72 (inset), 85 (bottom), 87, 105, 122, 123, 124,
  125, 130, 131, 132, 134, 137, 147, 151, 165, 167
Personal Narratives of John Russell Bartlett: *Horsehead Crossing 1849*, 11
Texas Parks & Wildlife: 71, 108, 133, 138 (top), 213
Texas State Library: 128
Title Insurance and Trust Company, Los Angeles: 95 (top)
United States Army: 158
University of Texas, Eugene C. Barker Texas History Center: 25, 28, 61, 64, 83,
  103, 138 (left), 154, 163
Wadsworth Antheneum, Hartford, Colt Collection: 10

7323